# MIGHTIER THAN THE SWORD

D0038976

## KATHLEEN ADAMS, M.A.

**WARNER BOOKS**

A Time Warner Company

Warner Books, Inc., 1271 Avenue of the Americas, New York, NY 10020

W A Time Warner Company

Printed in the United States of America

First Printing: June 1994

10 9 8 7 6 5 4 3 2 1

**Library of Congress Cataloging-in-Publication Data**
Adams, Kathleen, 1951–
    Mightier than the sword: the journal as a path to men's self-discovery/Kathleen Adams.
        p. cm.
    Includes bibliographical references.
    ISBN 0-446-39464-5
    1. Men—Psychology.   2. Diaries—Authorship.   3. Self-actualization (Psychology)—Problems, exercises, etc. I. Title.
    BF692.5.A          1994                                         93-42319
    158'.1'081—dc20                                                 CIP

*Book design by H. Roberts*
*Cover design and photography by Julia Kushnirsky*

"Journal keeping is one of the most effective and enjoyable ways we have of raising and extending awareness. MIGHTIER THAN THE SWORD offers marvelous insights as well as practical suggestions—a gem!"

—Jeremy Taylor, Unitarian-Universalist minister, author of *Where People Fly and Water Runs Uphill: Using Dreams to Tap the Wisdom of the Unconscious*

※

"Men—and women—who are ready to put down the sword, pick up the pen, and discover more about themselves can write for years with the ideas in this book. They will free and inspire your mighty pen!"

—Joyce Chapman, M.A., author of *Journaling for Joy* and *Live Your Dreams*

※

"Adams has devised a variety of novel and creative techniques to help unleash the writers' emotions and thoughts...helps guide us to rethink our basic values, our roles in the family and society, and our past....I will certainly recommend it to my students and friends."

—James W. Pennebaker, professor, psychology department, Southern Methodist University, author of *Opening Up*

※

Dedicated to my father
Dale Hartley Adams (1913–1991)
May your teachings live for seven generations

# CONTENTS

# ACKNOWLEDGMENTS

There are a great many people to whom I owe a great deal of gratitude. Without their assistance and support, this book could not have actualized.

I had the good fortune to be born into a family I'd choose all over again as friends. To my mom, Theda; my sisters, Susie and Cindy; my brothers-in-law, Mike and Leo; my grandmother, Goggie; my nieces, Jessica, Ricki, Amy, Kelly and Susanna; and my nephew Jake I offer my love and thanks. Although my father is no longer physically present he is very much alive in our hearts. It is to him this book is dedicated.

My women's group, Akasha, has now been together five years. Every week I enter a sacred space of unconditional acceptance, commitment and support. This book was conceived, carried and birthed in the love of my

Akasha partners, Jean Jameson, Andrea Hilgert and Thia Walser. My gratitude is boundless.

A circle of she-wolves, Patty Lucas, Laura Gryczen, Barbara Barstow and by rainbow connection Judi Walsh, offered safe haven to explore descents into the deep unknown. For the courage, commitment, strength and wisdom I've gained in our travels together, I offer a prayer and a howl.

Judi Walsh, Carl Kallansrud, Barbara Barstow, C. J. Pollara and Marta Hedde generously and expertly coached me through every stage of research and writing with patience, persistence and endless good humor. In the early stages, Dr. Gladys Kuoksa offered her considerable wisdom and expertise on research design, and Bruce Brooks offered research assistance and co-facilitation. Dr. Kathryn Fentress provided gentle guidance along an often bumpy road. In the final deadline push, Virginia Whitson's wise counsel kept the channels open.

My author friends know that this business of book writing is often hard, lonely work. For their stories, tips, encouragement, humor and support I thank Christina Baldwin, Tristine Rainer, Ellen Baker, Peggy Osna Heller, Kay Leigh Hagan, Joyce Chapman and Jessica Wulf.

My agent, Linda Barclay, once again sold a book on the strength of a concept. Warner Books once again placed faith in my ability to take a good idea and turn it into a manuscript. My editor, Colleen Kapklein, once again offered freedom and structure in just the right combinations.

Deep appreciation goes to the men's councils and men's movement leaders around the country who have embraced the concept of this book and acknowledged the need to which it speaks. Likewise, I am grateful to the places and people who were willing to sponsor, organize or facilitate men's journal workshops: Men's Association of Religious Science (MARS), Mile Hi Church, John Turak, Dick Gero, Joannah Merriman, Joe Cotter, Reverend Patty Lucas, Bill Stephenson, Bruce Brooks; in Canada, Judi Walsh, Jim McCaughey, Ross Bartleman, Ellen Campbell, That Other Bookstore and Dan-Elle Learning.

There would not have been a book at all were it not for the men. Nearly three hundred of them touched this work with their minds, hearts, lives and pens. To every one I offer my thanks. To those who contributed writings I am especially grateful. Their stories give this work its life and breath.

Finally I give thanks to God, from whom all pages flow.

# FOREWORD

The twentieth century has demanded a lot from American men. First there was World War I, then World War II, then the Korean War, the Cold War, the Vietnam War, the Persian Gulf War and several "skirmishes." To be effective and efficient in these wars and in earning a living, males had to be "toughened up" by parents, schools, churches, media, and the military. As they grew into adulthood, these males were expected to display characteristics of leadership, independence, toughness, courage, responsibility, and quiet stoicism. These traits became synonymous with manliness and played a major role in keeping our country free and our standard of living high.

Unfortunately, however, while millions of men in our country have had the traditional masculine traits drilled into their heads and hearts, they've received precious little training about the traditional feminine ways of being. Without the "feminine" qualities of patience, vulnerability, gentleness, compassion, and empathy, these men are destined to become emotionally unbalanced. Boys who grow up emotionally unbalanced in this way, especially those without a concerned, involved father, tend to feel insecure and often have a low self-esteem. These boys often attempt to make up for their insecurities by following the rules of manhood in an exaggerated fashion.

Thus, under such circumstances, "Be stoic and don't let your feelings get in the way of positive action" becomes "Don't ever cry or show your vulnerable emotions, no matter what." "Be strong enough to get the job done and don't give up too soon" becomes "Don't ever be weak, don't compromise, and never give up." "Be brave" becomes "Don't ever be scared, but if you are, never let anyone know." "Be capable of leading when necessary" becomes "Prove your manliness by controlling and dominating those around you." "Be a responsible provider" becomes "Prove your worth to bosses, coworkers, and wives by pleasing them and achieving at all costs."

After working with thousands of males in our country, I am convinced that a significant number of men have been so influenced by one or more of these exaggerated masculine rules that their ability to enjoy meaningful relationships or even life itself has been deeply diminished. Although following the manly code may have paved the way for men to achieve success in business, sports, or war, the toll on their wives, their children, their friends, their planet, and themselves has been unacceptable.

Millions of American men spend a lot more time trying to prove themselves than they do celebrating themselves. They spend more time feeling numb, anxious or angry than they do feeling joyful. To make matters worse, many of these men just go through the motions in their relationships. Because they can't be vulnerable and haven't developed the necessary communication skills, they are often unable to experience the deep inner satisfaction that should come from intimate relationships with wives, children, and friends. Instead, they spend much of their lives trying to cope with soul-wrenching isolation and loneliness.

Emotionally unbalanced men fall prey to very "unmasculine" feelings of inadequacy, anxiety, depression, and dependency. To avoid or to cope with these painful and embarrassing emotions, millions of men have turned to such manly solutions as excess work, alcohol, TV sports, food, sexual compulsions, and even aggression and violence. Unfortunately, these "solutions" not only don't work, they create more problems. I sincerely believe divorce, addictions, child abuse, suicide, crime, and pollution could all be reduced by 75 percent or more if men could just become a little more emotionally balanced.

This serious malady affecting so many American men must be addressed if our families and our nation are to flourish. Rather than blaming men, concerned people should make an honest attempt to understand why men behave as they do. Men and women must join together to find solutions to what has become an increasingly destructive problem. As a nation, we must raise our awareness of the negative effects of unbalanced gender conditioning. And we must find fresh ways to help the men who are already emotionally wounded. New tools, such as gender specific therapies, must be designed to assist these men as they try to develop healthier ways of thinking, feeling, and behaving.

Journaling is one of the tools proving to be very effective for helping men to balance and enrich their lives. While many men are uncomfortable confiding in others, they can, over time, learn to give a voice to their inner thoughts and feelings by writing regularly in their journals. In this way, journaling can become the bridge that links a man's hidden, inner self with his outer, social self. As his vulnerable self gradually surfaces in his writings, a man's awareness and acceptance of who he really is begins to emerge. As he learns to communicate with this vulnerable, essential part of himself, a man is more able to communicate compassionately with the vulnerable side of his wife, his children, and his friends. This process becomes the foundation of a healthier, more emotionally balanced man. It is through this kind of work that love for self and others becomes more of a reality than a fantasy.

After reading Kay Adams's *Mightier Than the Sword*, I am even more convinced that regular journaling can change men's lives. In fact, I am now introducing journaling into my men's therapy groups and am using it in my personal life.

For centuries, philosophers have said that the pen is mightier than the sword. This book proves their point.

—MARVIN ALLEN, M.A., psychotherapist and author of *Angry Men/Passive Men: Understanding the Roots of Men's Anger and Moving Beyond It* (formerly *In the Company of Men*). Marvin is also director of the Texas Men's Institute and chairman of the annual International Men's Conference.

# MIGHTIER THAN THE SWORD

# INTRODUCTION

T his book is quite literally the manifestation of a dream.

In September 1986 I had a dream in which a gathering of men informed me that I had a role to play in helping men communicate, reflect, grow and heal. I was given three specific tasks: *Your first task is to support us in doing our work. Your second task is to help us to know ourselves. Your third task is to help us teach each other.*

The first task was easy, and in the dream I said so. When I asked how I was to carry out the other two tasks I was told I would receive further instructions. Then I woke up.

A few days later I began teaching a class in process writing at Boulder Graduate School. To my great surprise, at a school where men comprised only 20 percent of the student body, the men in my class outnumbered the women three to one. For the first time in my journal career, I was able to facilitate and observe men's collective written voice. The relief and resonance the men expressed when writings were shared (*I know just what you're saying!* or *I've felt like that myself!* or *I thought I was the only man who experienced it that way!* or *That's the first time I've ever told anyone!*) touched us all at a very deep place.

Years passed. Journals remained my passion. I wrote two journal books, taught dozens of journal classes, facilitated hundreds of people as a journal therapist, read thousands of journal entries.

One day in late 1991, while trying to write a proposal for a book on clinical journal therapy, I developed a dreadful headache. I finally quit ignoring it and stretched out on my office couch to rest. As I drifted into an uneasy dream-state, I flashed on a story from Greek mythology about a terrible headache suffered by the god Zeus. Through an intricate series of psychological motivations and physiological accommodations, Zeus was gestating a baby in his forehead. His daughter Athena, goddess of wisdom and warfare, was about to be born.

> Retreating to the Triton River, Zeus screamed in great agony as his head finally went into labor. Zeus stooped down and between contractions begged [Hephaistos] to split his head open. Hephaistos dutifully brought down his ax. . . . The head immediately opened up, and out leaped a sprightly new goddess, full grown and (accounting for some of Zeus' agony) fully armed with crescent helmet,

breastplate, shield and spear. (Donald Richardson, *Greek Mythology for Everyone*)

In a kaleidoscopic dream-rush, an idea sprang forth full-grown from my head. A journal book offering men new ways to tell their own stories, in their own words, about their own issues. A book building bridges between intellect and emotion, outer and inner, head and heart, focus and vision. A book facilitating communication with self and others. A book offering practical, pragmatic assistance for relinquishing emotional armoring. In one exquisite moment of holographic insight and inspiration, I received the key message of this book: The pen is mightier than the sword.

Tumbling on the heels of this discovery was the memory of my 1986 dream. I recalled the men and their message: *Your second task is to help us know ourselves. You will receive further instructions.*

I sat up. My headache was gone. I returned to the computer and began anew. Three weeks later Warner Books accepted the proposal for *Mightier Than the Sword*, and I was launched on my own heroic journey.

I began this project knowing exactly how I wanted it to end, and with not a clue how to get there. In January 1992 I surveyed a thousand men on their experiences with and attitudes about personal growth, emotional healing, spiritual practice, "men's work" and reflective writing. Nearly three hundred responded, and a data base was born. From this initial pool my associate Bruce Brooks and I filtered through the men who expressed interest in local groups and workshops, those who wanted to take a home-study course and those who could arrange workshops or presentations in other cities.

The survey provided valuable demographic and psychographic information, as well as pinpointing individual and collective issues, journal successes and stoppers, experiences with psychological growth, and spiritual practices.

In the spring I began teaching men's journal workshops in Denver and Boulder. The home-study program came together. My fax machine began cranking out knee-deep ribbons. Suddenly I was immersed in the intimate writings and processes of dozens of men. The next time I take on a project of this magnitude, I'll remember to find some outside funding to finance research associates and office help. My biggest regret about the project is that there were so many men for whom participation was limited or not even initiated because my resources and stamina were stretched at every stage.

Much like a journal, the process was sometimes circuitous and baffling, sometimes brilliant and crystalline, always unexpected and never finished. From the beginning the work had a life force all its own. An entry from my journal during the summer of 1992 reads:

> The men's research has grown so much that it gets its own file cabinet drawer. I'm moved not only with the depth of the writing of the men in the study, but also with their insight, courage and confusion. Through their words and responses, the book begins to weave itself. Like a potter with a hunk of clay, I sense the beginnings of form; still, the clay shapes itself and I just guide the wheel. I do not know yet what the book will be like. But it knows, and sometimes it shares with me.

I'm no stranger to translating complex concepts and ideas into words. I used to write tax newsletters and business management books and psychiatric textbook chapters for a living. But the actual writing of this book holds the dubious honor of being my most difficult and challenging writing project to date. Through the miracle of holistic process, the book came together in the summer of 1993.

In his Foreword to my workbook, *The Way of the Journal: A Journal Therapy Workbook for Healing,* Walter Young noted, "This is the paradox and wonder of journals: What we write stands permanently, but only for the moment. It is not indelible, fixed or static. A journal entry is but an illuminated fragment of time, a way station between the past and future, a crystallized point on a continuum of change." I think of this book in much the same way. There is much more to be shared; once they found their writing voices, the men wrote on and on. The potential certainly exists for other books about men's reflective writing. The chapter on emotions, as just one example, could easily be expanded into its own book with rich case studies and illustrations.

Although I initially approached this project with ideas and schemata about gender differences in reflective writing, I found that the more I worked with men, the more I realized we're all dealing with the same stuff. To that end this book is completely appropriate for women, just as my previous two books, drawn predominantly from women's work, are equally applicable for men. The journal ladder discussed in chapter 5, for instance, is a theoretical construct I developed while working with post-traumatic stress-disordered women, and at first I thought its usefulness might be specific to that particular audience. However, when I applied it to the men's work

I realized that it also organically fits with areas of natural mastery associated with the masculine principle, such as structure, order, sequencing, discernment and decisiveness. Still later I realized that the journal ladder works because it works. It doesn't have anything to do with gender or diagnosis; it's just a solid theoretical base upon which to build a journal relationship.

The last task given to me in the dream was to help men teach each other. To this end I will continue to train qualified individuals to teach journal workshops in their own communities; write for information on the Instructor Certification Training available "live" in Denver or Toronto, or by home study on audiotape. My vision is circles of men, women, men and women, families and communities who gather to write and share and grow.

This book began with a dream, and it ends with one as well. As I wrote the last draft I dreamed that I stood before a room of men. A colleague rose to introduce me, but first he invited the men to give up their knives (swords). Wordlessly they surrendered knives of every size, utility and description. My friend collected them in a black tarp. I bowed my head in a gesture of silent respect for the courage to relinquish protection and defenses. When I looked up, the men had begun to write.

—KATHLEEN ADAMS, M.A., L.P.C.
The Center for Journal Therapy
P.O. Box 963
Arvada, CO 80001
New Moon, September 15, 1993

# How to Use This Book

This book is designed to give you practical, immediately useful ways to use a journal for personal growth, problem-solving, stress management, creative expression and a whole host of other applications. Although there is a developmental design to the book, each chapter stands alone, and the chapters need not be read in sequential order. The first part of the book is like ground school. You'll learn the basics: why men write journals, how to get started, what to do if you get stuck. You'll also get an entire toolbox of techniques to help add interest, variety and results to your journal, and a ten-rung ladder that will help you match techniques with desired outcomes. You'll learn how to blast through old messages or tapes about your writing ability. There's an inside peek at those secret little childhood diaries. Especially if you're new to journalkeeping, or if your journal results have been less than satisfying until now, you'll find this orientation helpful.

Feel free, however, to plunge right into the second section. Here you'll find explorations of some of the most prevalent issues of today's men: authenticity, identity, childhood wounds, fatherhood, emotions, values, dreams and spirituality. Through stories, case studies and the powerful writings of men you'll learn how to use your journal to approach these issues safely, sensitively and intelligently.

Men's writings are marked with this icon: Editing has been kept to an absolute minimum so that unique styles of expression can be preserved. Names have been changed and identifying characteristics altered unless the writer requested otherwise.

Each of the issues chapters contains a section called Pick Up Your Pen. This section is a menu of writing ideas designed to lead you into and through the processes discussed in the chapter. Part of the benefit, satisfaction and enjoyment of journal writing comes from learning how to create your own trail map.

You can approach Pick Up Your Pen in one of two ways. First, you can scan the suggestions and start with the ones that appeal to you most. Deepen your work by going back to the list and choosing again. With a little practice you'll become proficient at sensing how the journal ideas fit together like a mosaic. The second approach, to complete the Pick Up Your Pen section of any chapter in sequential order, is especially helpful when you want a detailed, comprehensive personal growth experience.

The difference between the two approaches is like the difference between shooting photographs of scenes or people and doing a photographic study of one scene or person. You'll be equipped with the tools to do both; you must choose where you wish to place your attention.

If you are in therapy or counseling, please show this book to your therapist and talk about incorporating your journal process into treatment. I have developed many resources for therapists and clients alike on journal writing as a therapeutic adjunct, so your therapist may want to contact me.

Some authors and workshop leaders are suggesting the practice of writing with your nondominant hand (your left hand if you are right-handed, and vice versa), usually as a way of freeing up creativity and/or the voice of the "inner child" or "inner teacher." It's true that this is an effective technique for accessing information that is not readily available in other ways. But it's a wild card; nondominant-handwriting seems to release whatever is below the surface of consciousness, and particularly when there is a history of emotional, physical or sexual trauma the practice can trigger some mighty unpleasant feelings, memories and assocations. If you're drawn to nondominant-handwriting, treat it with respect. Review the anchor of structure in chapter 4 (pages 49–52) before you experiment with this powerful and unpredictable device.

I encourage you to approach this book with a spirit of adventure and anticipation. You're about to embark on a marvelous journey of discovery. Here are the rules: (1) Date every entry; (2) be open to surprises; and (3) forget the other rules. I know you can write, and you'll know too as soon as you start writing.

*Part One*

# PICK UP
# YOUR PEN

## Chapter One
# MEET THE MEN

The men in this book are just like you. They are husbands, fathers, lovers, sons and brothers. They are colleagues, citizens, neighbors and friends. They do their best to be honest, ethical, authentic, responsible and conscious. Often they struggle. Sometimes they fail. They are real men living less than perfect lives. Like you, each grows and changes at his own pace, carving out his unique destiny in his individual way.

Each of them is writing the book that only he can author: the story of an individual life, captured with idiosyncratic wonder in the pages of a notebook.

William is at a crossroads. After nearly thirty years in the fast lane, he has achieved all the accoutrements of success: six-figure salary, corner office, CEO status, a getaway home. But William wants more. He doesn't want more money, status or power; he wants more peace of mind. More time with his wife and son. More time with himself. In his journal he arrives at a decision to leave his company and dance to the music of his soul.

Greg has a secret. He's lived with it all his life. He can't talk about it, and it never goes away. Every day he carefully dons his mask and goes out into the world, hiding his secret away so that no one will know. Sometimes his loneliness throbs like a bad tooth. His journal knows his secret and accepts it without judgment.

Steve's wife died a few years ago. His path through grief led him to men's retreats and groups, where he learned to accept the compassion and love of his brothers. Retired now, he finds new vitality in writing articles and poetry for the local and national men's press.

Hank teaches communication at a large university. Soon after his divorce, his ex-wife and two-year-old son moved a thousand miles away. Faced with the necessity of creating a long-distance relationship with a toddler, Hank discovered how much he had to learn about this important endeavor. His instruments of choice are the telephone and a journal written to and for his son.

One time Edward's father beat him so badly that he almost died. It was one of the last beatings; he was twelve and getting big enough to fight back. Now his father is old and frail. Sometimes when he lifts his father into the wheelchair Edward chokes on his conflicting emotions. Compassion comes in the pages of his journal.

Thomas has enjoyed a successful career as a writer. He was in a car accident last year and broke his neck. He's recovering, but it's a slow comeback, and disability doesn't cover all the bills. He lives in a tent south of town and writes at the public library.

Taylor is an art therapist. He counsels men dying of AIDS. The horror and anguish of their suffering eats at his soul. He paints and writes his way through the pain.

Al teaches school. His work is rich and satisfying. His love for his wife deepens and mellows with every year. They have a beautiful little boy. Al is grateful for his life. He only wishes his father had lived to see him grow into a man. In his journal, Al remembers his father and creates a legacy for his son.

Jerry's star is rising. He's successful, smart and talented. He has a beautiful wife and daughter. His image is impeccable. He wonders why he feels like a fraud. In his journal he takes an honest look at himself.

Mark is an alcoholic in recovery. One page at a time he prays to the God of his understanding for serenity, courage and wisdom.

Jeremy struggles to find the balance between intimacy and independence. His journal helps him chart the map of these unfamiliar waters.

Michael's childhood was far from perfect, but he tries to keep it in perspective. His deep desire is to have a loving adult relationship with his mother.

Jim has a sensitive streak that women appreciate and men often misunderstand. In his journal, he expresses his feelings without fear of judgment.

Daniel wants to write, but all his life people have told him he can't. In his journal he learns that they were mistaken.

Greg and Jeremy, Steve and Daniel are some of the men you will come to know through their honest and unedited writings. While it is true that some men avoid the mirror of the journal because it's painful to see their own reflections, there are others who dare to glimpse their own interiors. For them, the question is not, Can I bear to see? The questions instead are, How can I learn to look? What questions do I ask myself? And what do I do with the answers?

Listen and you will hear the collective grief over the confusion it is to be a man today. You will hear hope and courage. You will hear commitment to change and growth and healing, to ending violence and rescuing the earth and honoring the indwelling Spirit in all.

These are the stories of ordinary men living ordinary lives. What makes them so remarkable is that they are each so extraordinary. In the journal we are all sages and prophets. Uncap your pen, and your life tumbles out before you. I promise that you will be astounded by the wisdom and grace that are literally at your fingertips if you will only begin to write.

As a collection of intimate writings, these stories make powerful reading. They are offered here virtually untouched. Some excerpts have been abridged, but there has been almost no editing of actual content. There are two professional writers in the bunch; otherwise, these men do not consider themselves writers. In fact, most of them started out convinced they were not good writers.

If you do nothing more than experience the journals of your brothers, resonant healing will likely take place. But there is so much more. The story of your own life is waiting to be told. Through the suggestions and processes in this book you will learn how to tell that story in your own words, with your own voice.

You are not alone. There are men just like you who hurt, who grieve, who complain, who dream, who get confused, who celebrate, who strike out, who fall down and get up, who yearn for meaning and purpose. They have forged a path before you. Allow them to guide you along it. Lay down your sword. Pick up your pen. Your brothers await your story.

## PICK UP YOUR PEN

- If you are beginning a new journal, leave the first page of your notebook blank. Use it as a title page or simply to create a boundary.
- With which men's stories do you most identify? Why? In your journal, reflect on the similarities.
- Write a thumbnail sketch of yourself and your present life situation.
- Draw a line vertically down the middle of your page. On the left side, make a list of the things that would make up the best-case scenario about writing a journal. What do you hope to accomplish? What do you want to be, do, have, feel, experience in the pages of a journal? On the right, list what would happen in the worst-case scenario. What might get in your way? What hesitations or doubts do you have? What might stop you from achieving your best-case scenario?

## Chapter Two

# FOURTEEN REASONS TO WRITE A JOURNAL

There are probably as many reasons to write a journal as there are journal writers. Although this list is far from exhaustive, here are fourteen of the most common reasons why men write their lives. Each point is illustrated with excerpts from the journals of men, marked with this icon:

## *Read your own mind.*

When you write something down, you can literally read your own mind. You can externalize your thoughts, opinions, beliefs, and feelings into a form that is real and concrete. You can capture ideas, name feelings and preserve moments. You can talk to yourself on paper. You can even answer yourself!

Late at night when I'm having trouble sleeping, I often get up and open the pages of my journal and carry on a dialogue with my higher self. My higher self always goes right for the jugular and cuts through my bullshit rationalizations. My higher self doesn't waste time with me when I'm feeling sorry for myself and doesn't put up with excuses. It always encourages me to step out and get off of dead center. (Greg)

## Manage time and projects.

Once I asked ten people to name the possession kept on their person that they would be most upset if they lost. Six people said their day planners or appointment books. (Two said car keys, one said wallet, and a new mother said her baby.)

If you too live through your calendar, start thinking of it as a business journal. Imagine what else you could use it for. Productivity logs? Time inventories? Production schedules? Goal sheets? If you don't have a day planner system with sections for notes and planning, get a small notebook the same size as your appointment book and section it off yourself. You'll find that a minimal investment in time—as little as ten or fifteen minutes a day—can pay enormous dividends in increased efficiency, clarity and productivity.

A leading business school conducted a twenty-five-year follow-up study of its M.B.A. graduates. Measurements of success included income, executive status, company perks, and so on. They found that the top 13 percent all regularly followed a program of goal-setting and follow-up. The top 3 percent, which was doing significantly better than the next 10 percent, regularly did this in writing.

> Another notion just crossed my mind—does journaling assist or enable individuals to actually DO more or fulfill more intentions than individuals who do not journal? The journal then becomes the ACTION PLANNER that captures the essence of the goals or objectives without getting into prescriptive, perhaps limiting models that look good but don't implement well. Wouldn't it be nice to spend more time DOING and less time making the perfect PLAN. (Jim)

## Focus and clarify your desires.

Think of your journal as a high-powered microscope that magnifies certain "cells" of your life. When the inner workings are revealed through the lens of the journal, you have "useful knowing"—information that can be used to nourish your individualized desires and purposes.

For example, a simple sentence-completion exercise that begins "Success means . . ." helps clarify your personalized definition of success. It may be very different from the definitions of your coworkers, sales manager or father. This is useful knowing.

Or say that you go to a networking breakfast, recap your experience in a five-minute writing sprint and discover that the contact that had the most impact on you was with an elderly man in a wheelchair who reminded you of your wise grandfather. This might tell you that the breakfast was a pleasant social encounter but not an efficient use of business time, or it might tell you to spend more time with your grandfather. Whatever you glean is useful knowing that supports the attainment of your own desires.

Writing brings about a crystallization of thought. It brings together scattered alternatives onto a piece of paper or a notebook. Often the process of writing— mind to paper—brings about an awareness which was not previously experienced, even though the individual ideas were in the mind. A kind of gestalt takes place. (Matthew)

## Manage stress and improve overall health.

Research psychologist James Pennebaker has studied the impact of writing on health. His studies show that subjects who write about emotionally sensitive issues for as little as fifteen minutes a day over four consecutive days show increased immune system functioning, decreased hypertension and overall improved physiological response to stress. That's a pretty powerful wallop for an hour's worth of writing! In *Opening Up: The Healing Power of Confiding in Others*, Pennebaker states:

[A]ctively holding back or inhibiting our thoughts and feelings can be hard work. Over time, the work of inhibition gradually undermines the body's defenses. Like other stressors, inhibition can affect immune system function, the action of the heart and vascular systems, and even the biochemical workings of the brain and nervous systems. In short, excessive holding back of thoughts, feelings and behaviors can place

people at risk for both major and minor dis-
eases. . . . Confronting our deepest thoughts and
feelings can have remarkable short and long term
health benefits. Writing . . . about upsetting things can
influence our basic values, our daily thinking patterns
and our feelings about ourselves. Not disclosing our
thoughts and feelings can be unhealthy. Divulging
them can be healthy.

## Create community.

There is power in telling your story to a listening
audience. Whether you are your own audience of one or
have any number of attentive others, consider reading
your writings aloud. It is healing to be heard. Listening to
your own words in your own voice often brings up
insights and awarenesses that otherwise would go
unnoticed. It's also healing to hear the stories of others.
There is a universality to the shared experience that is
healing for everyone involved.

The writings of the men in the study give me great
insights into my own life. I feel less of an outsider
in the "male" world. I guess this is true because the
written words carry an honesty and reality from inside
that might not otherwise make it to the outside. (Gary)

In 1992 Joe Cotter, a certified instructor of The
Center for Journal Therapy, led a journal group at the
Colorado State Prison in Canon City. The prisoners were
so moved by the combination of reflective writing and

group process that they lobbied for an extension when the group came to an end.

> I am thrilled to be a part of this group. I feel your questions cause me to open some long-closed doors. I think the group today has provided a few new paths for my journal and reaffirmed the value of my continuing this writing process. Hearing what others are writing opens doors between us fellow prisoners. (Sam)

## Identify and explore feelings.

I've read a file cabinet full of journals while researching this book, and it sure doesn't seem to me that men have trouble accessing their feelings. Their writings may evidence some difficulties identifying, communicating or appropriately acting on feelings, but there's no shortage of emotion in men's journals.

Men's journals show that if they had a safe place to identify and explore feelings with other men, they'd do it in a heartbeat. Men's journal groups provide simultaneous disclosure and detachment. Raw, honest feelings can be written first and shared later. The time lapse offers useful distance. Shyness and self-consciousness abate. Feelings are approached with respect and curiosity.

> My journal gives me permission to release feelings that are swimming around inside of me without putting labels of "good/bad" or "un/acceptable" on them. It's safe to do this because it's just me and the paper. Everything I write is okay. The journal doesn't judge what I put on it. It just accepts all that flows out.

What a releasing feeling! The next step is communicating with others vs. just my journal paper and I can begin to share my feelings with them. Challenging! Scary! Exciting! (Gary)

## Retrieve and heal the past.

Woundings are timeless. A painful experience is imprinted in cellular memory as happening in the present moment, with all the intensity of the original experience. To heal, old wounds must be detoxified and cleansed, and the timelessness must be interrupted by placing the event in a larger context. This can be painful and frightening. The journal is a safe and nurturing environment in which to do the hard work of emotional recovery.

Something not many people know about me is the words one of my college advisors said to me in 1966: "You aren't as good as your marks and your own opinion of yourself indicate!" This statement haunts me. I'm constantly nibbling away at myself wondering if I'm really not "as good." The self-doubt seems to be a shadow that's always present in varying degrees of intensity. I can't seem to let go of this 10-second snapshot of life that happened 26 years ago! (Jim)

## Discover and uncover resources.

A journal quickly takes on its own personality and becomes like a wise friend offering a running commentary on your decisions, plans, events and feelings. Before long you'll begin to notice the presence of qualities and resources that haven't been getting air time.

I find my journal has a life of its own that does not fit my original, traditional notions of what a journal is. It is more of a compendium of thoughts and feelings that identify themselves in writing. Through writing I am realizing a richer and more rewarding life for myself. I am also finding out that I am much stronger and more resilient than I would have previously thought. I'm also more aware of the possibilities available to me. This has been a significant gift and a major life turning point. Nice to see such far-reaching results from such a simple tool as writing. (Anthony)

## Practice communication and relationship skills.

Any new learning takes practice, and learning how to create and participate in intimate, meaningful relationships is no exception. Like a Broadway show that rehearses in another city before opening in New York, the journal becomes a "behavioral rehearsal"—a practice ground for articulating ideas and emotions before they are revealed.

Men have precious few opportunities to pour our hearts out, or even practice doing it. The journal lets me practice creating relationship and gives me courage to become conscious and objectify what's going on inside. The paper and pen are utterly silent and accepting. I can say things on paper that it would take me months or years to work up courage to say, to even my most trusted friend. And it doesn't cost me a thing. (Frank)

## *Build bridges from the outer to the inner.*

Journals are like bridges that span the distance from the head to the heart and from the outside to the inside. It is widely acknowledged that men in our society have been acculturated to place high value on the exterior world, the world of matter. It is only now, in the waning years of the twentieth century, that men are turning inside and seeking out the interior world, the world of instinct and intuition. The journal provides a forum for willing self-exploration.

> I learn things about myself when I write. I am always surprised if I let myself "follow the pen," i.e. let my mind flow out of the tip of the pen without censure. More of me emerges than I ever realized was there. (Gary)

## *Extend your therapy hour.*

In my workshops on journal therapy, I invite clinicians to tell me what they notice when their clients write journals. The number one response: Clients who write make better use of the therapy hour. Number two: They connect with feelings more easily and with less disruption. Number three: They seem to move through therapy more quickly. You may want to ask your therapist if you can share selections from your journal during your therapy hour.

> My journal was a frequent help during a period in which I felt very wounded, betrayed by my wife. I

was devastated. I started seeing a psychologist and found that I never had time to "wring myself out" fully with him. At home I would sit by the hour and write unsent letters to him, sharing my heart, squeezing myself to the max. (Edward)

## *Work the twelve steps.*

Each of the twelve steps of Alcoholics Anonymous and other recovery programs is enhanced by writing, and your journal is a safe and private place for the self-examination inherent in the individual steps. Additionally, your journal can serve as a bridge into a new lifestyle, a place to ventilate the restlessness, irritability and discontent of early-stage recovery, and a record for the future of how sobriety is achieved and maintained one day and one page at a time.

I got started with a journal when my AA sponsor shoved a notebook at me and told me to start writing every time I started craving. It worked. At first I just wrote about the craving itself—how bad I wanted a drink or a line—but after a while I noticed I was writing about what was happening that led up to the craving. After a while longer I started figuring things out, like which feelings went with which craving. It helped a lot to go back and read my journal and see where I'd been. When I first got clean and sober things changed so fast I couldn't always keep up with myself. Writing it all down helped me feel more in control. (Mark)

## Tell your story.

"We are storytelling animals," says Sam Keen in *Your Mythic Journey*. "To be a person is to have a story to tell." The mystics say that God created man because He loves a good story. Our stories define us individually as well as tribally. Without them we feel uprooted.

> Men are in trouble. Only men can tell other men what it means to be a man. Only when we are happy with who we are can we reach out with something to give. Man is a social animal. We instinctively band together to tell stories. We die when we separate ourselves or remain silent. Men are dying now. It is time for us to band together—tribally—to take care of each other again. (Greg)

## Explore spirituality.

The invitation to look inward carries with it the imprint of the Soul's journey. As the poet Rainer Maria Rilke suggests in *Letters to a Young Poet*, you can learn to love the questions themselves, and you may find that the answers are revealed moment by present moment.

> The most appealing thing about journal writing is that I tap a deeper level of my consciousness by writing. I am astounded by what surfaces. . . . My journal is my guide, my teacher, my mentor. It is the vehicle through which I explore my path of personal growth, inner searching and spiritual evolvement. It is

the way-shower, the wise elder whose counsel I seek. (Tykye)

Of course this list could go on and on. Other reasons to write include building self-confidence, exploring creativity, solving problems, providing relief from everyday stress, making sense of the present and finding balance. Whatever reason you have for writing now, it's likely that it will change and grow as you do.

> Initially I wrote to keep track of my experiences. But gradually over the years, my journal has become a friend with whom I share my struggles and successes. (Matthew)

## PICK UP YOUR PEN

- In your journal, explore which of these reasons you relate to most. Why? What reasons don't interest you? Why not?
- Marking up a book with underlines, highlights or marginal notes is sort of like writing a journal. Go ahead and mark up this book. Put today's date right here:

TODAY'S DATE_____

- When you select a journal process from this book, jot the date in the margin. That will help you retrieve the entry at some future point when you want to check your progress and growth.
- If you only establish one habit in your journal, let it be

this one: Date your entries with the month, day and year.

- You can also mark time in your journal in other ways: day of week, time, location, weather, this day in history, front-page headline, sports score.

## Chapter Three

# PREFERENCES

Quite a few years ago, upon the occasion of my promotion to the position of editorial vice president of a business publishing company, I bought a rolltop desk. My writer fantasies had changed over the years; I no longer pined for a garret in Sausalito or a teepee in Santa Fe. I did, however, pine for a rolltop desk. Those sensuous curves, that mysterious wooden veil, that hidden wildness, those clever cubbyholes . . .

The desk arrived on a Thursday, and I was so excited I took Friday afternoon off. For two days I organized in miniature, squirreling sections of my life away in tiny slots and drawers. Finally, on Sunday afternoon, I sat down to write. I lugged my Selectric typewriter over, set it down, and . . . hmmmm . . .

The typewriter didn't fit. It was too wide to nestle between the cubbyholes. A good three or four inches of

31

machine hung over the front edge. The chair wasn't high enough, so my hands cocked at a strange uphill angle as I typed, causing my palms to rest heavily on the extended lip. This in turn caused the typewriter to teeter precariously. It threatened to dump into my lap with every carriage return.

So much for my Selectric; I'd just write by hand. But the drama continued. I couldn't get the lamp adjusted to shine inside the desk, my right elbow kept bumping into a bank of cubbyholes, and it kept getting worse. I ended up writing at the dining-room table with my feet propped up on a swivel chair, just as I always did.

My rolltop desk is a beautiful piece of furniture, and I love having it. I keep my canceled checks in the cubbyholes and my passport in a tiny drawer, but I wouldn't write at that desk on a bet.

The point of all of this is that it doesn't much matter what you write a journal in or on, but it does matter whether it feels good to you.

Whenever I see new journal therapy clients who haven't yet started writing, I offer them a notebook. "Do you want wide lines or narrow lines?" I ask. About a quarter say wide, and a quarter narrow. The other half say, "I don't care" or "It doesn't matter." To which I say, "Oh yes, you do/it does." Then I open up two notebooks, put them side by side. "Choose," I say. They always do. The preference for wide lines or narrow lines (or blank) is, I think, encoded in the DNA, like the preference for mustard or catsup (or plain). The following first entry in Carter's journal shows decided preferences:

> On a less than positive note—I hate this notebook. I hate this pen. It bleeds so goodbye pen. [In different ink] I hate this notebook because (a) it isn't made from recycled paper (b) it doesn't have a double spiral (c) the

cover is wimpy (d) there is a stupid white unicorn on the front. It isn't sturdy enough. It won't survive bashings. But it was all I could find. I just wanted to say that I hate it. So it's temporary. Until I can go get a new one. [Only a few more pages were filled.]

Often in the second week of a new group I'll bring a stack of journals. There are books of all descriptions: loose-leaf notebooks, elegant leather-bound books, spirals, appointment books, parchment pages, yellow foolscap tablets, tiny-lined diaries, sketchbooks, handmade papers, a shoe box stuffed with notes and clippings. I spread them in the middle of the circle and invite everyone to explore. They're encouraged to speak their comments out loud.

- I hate this rigid binding! It's stiff.
- I like the way these thick pages feel.
- I don't like blank pages. I need lines.
- This one's too small. I feel cramped.
- The fabric cover is cheerful.
- I like the smell of leather, but the book is too nice to write in.
- My spiral notebook is just fine with me!
- Hey, I didn't think I'd like this one, but I do.

There are lots of choices. Each has pros and cons. Shop around and try different things out until you learn your own tastes and preferences.

*Handwritten books or notebooks.* You can't beat the portability; writing by hand allows you to add to your journal anytime, anyplace. Most start-up journalers find spiral or three-ring notebooks to be less intimidating than blank bound books.

If you like blank books, you'll find them in sizes ranging from shirt-pocket to oversized artist sketchbooks, at prices from six to more than sixty dollars. Covers are a lot more unisex than they were even a few years ago. Bandelier Designs gets my vote for best selection of reasonably priced ($14 to $20) books featuring recycled paper, blank or wide-lined pages, and hip natural fabric covers.

Handmade books are treasures, and there's a whole network of book artists who will customize any type of blank book you want. A chiropractor in San Francisco carves rubber stamps into images of archetypes and petroglyphs and makes journals stamped with visual soul food. A bookbinder in rural Virginia crafts hand-dyed, hand-stitched, hand-painted leather books made to last two hundred years. A woman in Boulder creates journals that feature handmade paper, scented oils (eucalyptus, sandalwood, cinnamon, and so on), visual/tactile treats and other sensory pleasures. Journal artists create gourmet books filled with originality and craftsmanship.

For your first blank books, though, I recommend something on the modest end of the scale. Quill Mark, available at nearly every greeting card store, makes a book with perforated pages that you can tear out if you don't like what you've written.

*Computer or word processor.* Prime-time television's whiz-kid doctor, Doogie Howser, closed each episode with an entry in his computer journal, which no doubt gave word-processed journals a boost. Many find keyboarding neater, faster and less tedious than handwriting. Neurologically, the action of both hands on the keyboard may contribute to whole-brain functioning. A three-ring notebook with dividers provides take-along storage for hard copies. Portable laptop systems offer flexibility. You can even get journal management software programs. For privacy, use a security password.

Disadvantages: If you're not a fluid typist, you can quickly lose your train of thought. There's a big temptation to edit or correct as you go, which interrupts spontaneity and concentration. Some people overcome this by turning the monitor off and typing on a blank screen, but they have the distraction of not being able to see what they've written.

Computers also give you access to bulletin boards on computer networks, and they are filling a unique journal-keeping niche. I have no direct experience with bulletin boards myself, but James Pennebaker says in *Opening Up:*

> Perhaps the most interesting development in the letter-writing world has been the computer bulletin board. Individuals can write long letters or short notes proclaiming their views on politics, physics, or love. What makes computer bulletin boards so intriguing is that people's letters can be anonymous. Bulletin boards, then, are a little like talking to someone on an airplane. Consequently, people often disclose some of their very deepest feelings. Unlike in the airplane situations, however, since everyone is invisible, there are often remarkably hostile interchanges. Particularly striking is the phenomenon of flaming, wherein a computer writer will brutally insult another person. Indeed, it is quite common for one person who might disclose a deeply personal experience to be assailed by another for being too sentimental or phony.

*Voice journals.* Hand-held microcassette tape players are perfect for the person on the go who just can't find time to write. They capture dreams upon awakening, thoughts during rush-hour commutes, musings before falling asleep or after a workout. As a bonus, you can hear yourself think; inflections and phrasings remain intact. The revival of storytelling bodes well for audio journals. Video/audio journals create multimedia family history.

Journalkeepers who live with blindness, cerebral palsy and paralysis report that voice journals are effective and that most techniques developed for written journals are adaptable to the oral form. Having heard the results, I would have to agree.

It is hard to retrieve voice journal entries. Transcription is labor-intensive, and cataloguing is cumbersome. Privacy is easily jeopardized. If you're drawn to voice journals, you'll probably find a way around these obstacles. Share your knowledge!

*Personal and environmental preferences.* Little things do count, and they're easy to gratify. Go on a field trip to the office supply store and try out the pens. When you find an everyday pen you like, buy a box.

There are a hundred small decisions that add to your physical comfort and sensory pleasure. Do you prefer writing inside or outside? Early or late? Alone or with others? For ten minutes or an hour? At home or away? Music? Coffee? Comfortable and deep writing is often contingent on such seemingly innocuous details.

## PICK UP YOUR PEN

- Describe your ideal journal.
- Which of the suggestions or ideas in this chapter appeal to you?
- Experiment with different environments, settings, props, and so on.

## Chapter Four

# EIGHT ANCHORS FOR JOURNALS AND LIFE

F or every man who has easily befriended his journal, who engages with it as helpmate and companion on the journey, there are many more whose
attempts to keep a journal have been met with frustration
or a sense of personal failure. The men in this book grap-
pled with some of these stumbling blocks:

- not knowing how to get started
- not knowing what to write about
- skipping days and then not being able to catch up
- starting and stopping, over and over
- lack of time
- feeling stuck or blocked
- discomfort with the feelings that come up
- feeling angry, guilty, depressed or like a failure
- losing interest
- getting sidetracked

When you're experiencing any of these common difficulties, your journal can loom like a black cloud. It can remind you of every other self-management agenda that you "shoulda/woulda/coulda" done and that you didn't, wouldn't or couldn't sustain.

Good news! Dropping a few simple anchors helps you troubleshoot most of the frustration, struggle and difficulty that comes from "journal block." With these anchors in place, you'll dramatically increase the satisfaction of your journal relationship.

## Permission

The anchor of permission allows you to free yourself of rigid or unrealistic notions of how you should be writing. You can divest yourself of the expectations that your journal be worthy of publication, or that you write every day, or that you get results every time. The anchor of permission means that you can keep what you write or throw it away. You can quit writing if you're bored or tired, even if you're not finished. You can follow the muse wherever it leads you, even if you started out with a whole different agenda in mind. You can share what you write or keep it private.

Developing the anchor of permission means you know your preferences (see chapter 3) and you indulge yourself in them. It also means you stay open to shifts in style or taste. For years I wrote exclusively in spiral notebooks—the "79-cent therapist" I referred to in my first book, *Journal to the Self: 22 Paths to Personal Growth*. Sometime in 1991 I switched to lovely handmade bound books, each its own work of art. Last year I used a computer. Now I'm back to blank books. Your journal will change as you change. Let it happen.

Permission means that you let yourself have what Virginia Satir called the "five freedoms," to know what you know, feel what you feel, believe what you believe, experience what you experience, want what you want. One of the prevailing themes in men's groups revolves around the absence of one or more of these freedoms: "I wasn't allowed to show my true feelings, so I learned to stuff them." "In my family, it wasn't okay to say what was on my mind." "My opinions didn't matter." In your journal, you can show your true feelings. It is okay to say what's on your mind. You can listen to yourself precisely because your opinions do matter.

Permission releases judgments. With this anchor you acknowledge yourself as "perfectly imperfect"—a traveler on a journey who adapts to changing circumstances and environments. You allow yourself your differences. You release yourself from expectations that your progress match external or internal barometers of "fast" enough or "good" enough. All parts of yourself are worthy of time and attention—even the parts that you find unappealing, shameful or ugly. Effective, useful communication with these parts of yourself can flourish in the pages of your journal when permission is anchored.

If you want to share your writing, this anchor also reminds you to obtain permission from your intended audience. Ask if the person wants to hear or read your journal. When you ask permission to share, you avoid placing your audience and yourself in awkward or uncomfortable situations. Don't take it personally if you're turned down. Some people aren't comfortable with the intimacy of a shared journal. Others may not be able to tolerate hearing your raw emotion or unvarnished truth. Understand that their choice is due to their own experiences and most likely has nothing to do with you.

## Balance

A journal without balance is like a car with a leaky tire: Any momentum that gets built up is quickly depleted. When your journal is out of balance you:

- stop and start a lot
- notice all your writing sounds alike
- feel restless, anxious or edgy when you think about writing
- sometimes have to force yourself to write
- don't feel you are getting anywhere
- feel bored with writing or with your journal or with yourself

(Note: If you're not experiencing these symptoms, good for you! Whatever you're doing is working. You can skip this section.)

Imbalance happens in the journal when some aspects of your life are overemphasized and others are underemphasized. For example, you write down your thoughts and opinions, but feelings are left in the dark. Or you describe your outer world to the exclusion of your inner world. Perhaps you record your actions, but you're quiet about your reactions. If your journal is imbalanced in this way, you might consider your writing lifeless or dull. You may become frustrated or discouraged, since you seldom achieve a satisfying depth.

Conversely, your journal may contain only the drama of your life. You may only write when you're in emotional crisis, or when internal pressure threatens to blow the lid off. Especially if you are working through trauma, your writing may become repetitive and circular. This type of imbalance is often accompanied by a sense of dread or unease when you think about writing. Every time you think about your journal, your response is something like "Oh, yuck. If I write I'll feel worse. I'll be in touch with all my pain and anger. I don't want to write." It's little wonder: If you only write at emotionally volatile times, or about emotionally traumatic subjects, in effect you're getting negatively conditioned to the journal process. You can troubleshoot this by writing about pleasant or amusing things, too.

The solution to journal imbalance is straightforward. Deliberately and consciously seek out the opposite end of your polarity. Here are some suggestions:

- A balanced life gives attention to mind, body, heart and spirit. If your journal feels imbalanced, it's likely that your life does too. Choose one area of underfocus and boost it with journal check-ins.
- If your journal feels boring or dull, let your creative side out. Write poems. Draw pictures. Tell stories. Daydream.
- If your journal feels scattered, focus on one thing. Take one area of your life and make a plan. List action steps. Set a goal, and note progress toward it. If you can't commit to something big, commit to something small.
- If your journal only captures the high drama in your life, pretend you are a highly paid consultant who has

been called in to stop the chaos. How do you "catas-
trophize"? Call yourself on it!

- If your journal only logs external events, notice internal responses. Listen to your inner voices. Dialogue
with your different parts.
- Joy, humor and gratitude are three excellent ways to
add balance to your journal. What was the best thing
that happened to you today? Who or what do you feel
grateful for or appreciative of? When did you last
laugh, and what prompted it? Cut out cartoons and
mount them in your journal. Doodle. Write prayers.
Copy inspiring or comforting quotations.
- A little balance goes a long way. You needn't alter
your style so radically that you no longer recognize
your journal.

## Privacy

This anchor reminds you to develop the habit of
respecting privacy and boundaries—your own and those
of others. One of the biggest stoppers to effective
personal writing is the concern that someone will violate
privacy and read your journal without permission. There
are some easy, practical and effective steps you can take
to troubleshoot this concern.

Imagine that you're in the break room at work. On
the table is a yellow spiral notebook with a slightly dog-
eared cover. No one in the room recognizes it. You flip
open the front cover to see if there's any identification.
Nope. Just a full page of writing, and even though you're
not really reading it, your eyes fall on enough key words

to know not only who it belongs to—but also your coworker's prevailing mood, crisis or gripe.

Now imagine that it's your yellow spiral notebook on the break room table. Many "violations" aren't at all intended to be invasions of privacy; they're just natural consequences. Which doesn't make it any less uncomfortable when it's your journal that's seemingly up for grabs!

A simple solution: Leave the first page of any new journal blank. This serves as a barrier between your private thoughts and anyone else's eyes. You may want to put your phone number with a request to call if the notebook is found. You can also include a message or reminder to anyone who might pick up your journal without your knowledge. This can range from "PRIVATE—KEEP OUT!" to "Read at your own risk" to "Work in process." One of my favorite disclaimers puts the responsibility for boundary violation squarely on the shoulders of the invading party:

> Please respect my privacy. And if you do happen to read this, don't tell me about it. I don't want to know! (Jeremy)

Other ways to protect your privacy: If you write on computer, you can protect your journal files with a password. Or you can keep your journal in a locking briefcase, file cabinet or car trunk.

If you live in a household with reasonable people, often all that's necessary is a direct, clear, assertive request: "I'm writing a journal. This is what it looks like. If you happen to see it lying around, I'd appreciate it if you'd leave it alone. Will you agree to do that?"

Most intentional violations of privacy are symptomatic of a much deeper communication issue. Journals get read because spouses, lovers, parents, sometimes even children, fear there is something they haven't been told, or told truthfully. They act on this fear by invading private space. Sometimes their worst fears are confirmed; sometimes not. Reading someone else's journal almost always boomerangs. Once in a great while I'll hear a story of how illicit journal-reading opened the door for meaningful communication, but infinitely more often it's a giant step toward disaster in a relationship.

People who write journals are much less likely to invade the journals of others, because they have a sense of what that would feel like. Invite others in your household to participate in journalkeeping, and make house rules about respecting privacy. You can also suggest a community journal cocreated by family members; or a dialogue journal between partners or parents and children. These interactive journals are kept in a prearranged place and become ongoing dialogues, family scrapbooks or forums for debate over emotionally charged issues.

## Honesty

The journal is a mirror for the authentic, honest self. Your own truth is not your enemy, and a journal is a good place to start befriending your own truth.

Secrets are sneaky. They're like those bugs that live on the underside of a fallen tree: Expose them to the light, and they'll scuttle right into a knothole. That's how it is with secrets in your journal. Give them a little light, and they dive deeper underground than before.

I've been writing journals for more than thirty years, and there are still some neurotic little secrets that I'm loath to commit to paper. Why? Because when I acknowledge them in writing—when I tell myself the truth—then right there before me in my own black-and-white hand is the evidence of my inability or unwillingness to change my lifestyle, behavior or mind.

The journal documents the process of change, which is seldom linear. Rather, change is like a cha-cha: Some steps forward, some steps in place, some steps back. Although the backward steps can feel like relapses or failures, they really are not; they're just part of the dance.

The anchor of honesty helps you remember to document the backward steps as well as the forward and in-place steps. When you tell yourself the truth, you can learn from your experiences. When I was quitting smoking, I carefully noted every day that I successfully went without a cigarette. I filled page after page with resisted temptations, new awarenesses and behavioral substitutions, but on the not-infrequent occasions when I bummed a cigarette from a coworker or (gulp) swiped a butt from an ashtray, I was too ashamed to confess it. As a result, my data gathering was incomplete. I had no way of relating my backward steps to the specific vulnerabilities of my day.

All that is required of you is to be as honest as you possibly can be at any given moment. This sometimes means that you might write, "There's something going on, but I can't write about it right now." It might even mean that for a while you write in code, assigning key words or phrases to particular life situations or events.

Here are some springboards to help with the honesty anchor. When you notice yourself avoiding, *stop right there*, drop down a line, and write as fast as you can.

* What I really want to write about is—
* What does my heart say?
* I'm aware that I'm avoiding—

## Silence

"As it is in poetry, silence is a part of the form," writes Tristine Rainer in *The New Diary*. "The silence in diaries can speak as eloquently as words."

People sometimes misdiagnose journal silence as a cause for concern or judgment. You may go for several days, or weeks, or even months without writing and tell yourself, "I tried to write a journal, but I couldn't keep it up. I guess I'm just not cut out for journalkeeping." While it's true that journals are not the tool of choice for everyone, it's also true that many people give up too soon. Before you jump to conclusions, consider that silence may be a valuable messenger.

There are several reasons why journals fall silent. One is simply that life gets in the way. Overcommitment of time and energy makes it difficult to eke out enough resources for the necessities, much less the extras like reflective writing.

If you are experiencing this type of silence, it's a good reminder to check in with your level of stress. Are you meeting obligations to others at the expense of your responsibilities to yourself? If so, your journal can be part of a system of checks and balances. Try some of the quick writing techniques from chapter 5 to touch base with yourself, organize your tasks, plan your follow-up and inventory your resources. This on-the-run type of journalkeeping can often be incorporated into your time management planner or appointment book.

Another type of silence comes from inarticulacy—not knowing what to say or how to say it. This silence is often rooted in emotions such as anxiety, sadness or shame. There's often a fear that writing will open up an uncontainable Pandora's box of complicated, difficult feelings and issues.

The message in the silence of inarticulacy is to use the journal toolbox and ladder (chapter 5) and useful knowing about emotions (chapter 13) to select an approach that predicts success. With a little experience and practice, you'll become proficient at choosing methods that will give you a concrete sense of progress and accomplishment.

A third type of silence comes when there temporarily are no words. This silence often falls in the midst of a writing process, when you find yourself staring out the window, daydreaming, or doodling in the margins. The temptation is to decide that you have lost your train of thought, and that therefore your writing session must have come to its own end. This silence also comes when you go for days or weeks without picking up your journal, even though you have the time and perhaps even the desire to write.

When you find yourself in this type of silence, consider the possibility that something is probably happening beneath the surface that is not yet ready to be expressed. The invitation is to stay with the silence. It is often through sitting in silence waiting for answers that answers come. You may experience waves of boredom, restlessness, impatience, doubt, worry or paralysis. Let these waves move over and through you. If you can, write your way through them. If not, then just sit. When you are ready to break your own silence, it is likely that you will do so with eloquence, passion and inspiration.

## Attention

I once had a meditation teacher who would say, "What has a front, has a back." The other side of silence is attention.

When you give attention to your journal, you accept it as a part of your ongoing lifestyle and a useful tool in your self-management toolbox. Although it is not necessary (or even desirable) to become rigid, it's helpful if you can make a basic commitment to your journal exploration. Remember, if you can't commit to something big, commit to something small. You certainly don't have to write every day, or for an hour at a time. You might want to start with a commitment to give attention to your journal two or three times a week. If you're working on a specific project or issue, you might want to check in more frequently, but for shorter periods of time. During the months when writing this book was my full-time job, I started every day with a written meditation and ended every day with a summary of my progress. In between I dialogued with the book, kept a running to-do list, noted my angst and frustration, clustered chapter outlines and used my journal to organize and manage my life. Do I normally spend that much time with my journal? Not a chance!

The anchor of attention also calls you to pay attention to the subtle synchronicities of your life. There is meaning to be found in seemingly random events. Like dreams, these little webs of nuance can be elusive. Noting them allows you to find the connections and bridges between your inner and outer worlds and between your mundane tasks and your higher purpose.

Buddhism advocates the practice of "mindfulness," in which the mind chooses a focal point—the breath, a prayer, a flower—and attends to that one thing only. You can practice mindfulness, or attention, in your journal by focusing and writing about only what you perceive through one of your senses. You can focus on gratitude and list all blessings. You can focus on your body and scan each joint, muscle group, organ in turn. As meditation writer Joan Steadman notes:

> The benefits of this practice are many. To name a few: Stress is reduced, efficiency is increased, insight is sharpened. These results occur because, as the mind is one-pointed, there is no room for mental clutter, and we can now perceive more clearly.

## Structure

Paradoxically, structure creates movement. When you're stuck, this anchor gets you going again. Structure also sidesteps many of the most common stumbling blocks of journalkeeping: Not enough time, too much emotion, not sure how to start, don't want to get in too deeply.

When you incorporate structure into your journal, your writing processes have well-defined boundaries and clearly sequenced tasks. You choose writing techniques to accomplish specific outcomes. Structure creates an underlying form and order for your journal. Although you will never be able to predict what you will write, you'll come to know what to expect, what to invest in the way of time, energy and outcome.

Does this anchor inhibit or impede creativity? Not at all. If anything, it enhances creativity. It's easier to walk down hallways than through walls, and your creative energy also follows the easiest path, the path of least resistance. Once the foundation is in place, you can build anything you want on top of it.

Build structure in your journal by incorporating predictability into your writing environment. Create your own writing rituals or ceremonies. Experiment until you find what you like, and change your routine when it starts feeling stale. I've had the same five compact discs playing nonstop for about ten days now. It's my book-writing music. Some day soon I'll change it. Last year I only wrote with Cross fountain pens. In high school I went through a stage where I only wrote with a purple Lindy stick pen on a Big Chief tablet, and to this day a purple pen and a Big Chief tablet make me want to write bad poetry.

Your writing ritual might be as uncomplicated as making a pot of coffee or lighting a candle or sitting in the same chair at the dining-room table. Your journal structure might be as simple as using lined paper instead of blank paper. Or setting aside the same hour every Tuesday. Or always using a seventy-page spiral notebook with a red cover.

In chapter 5 you'll learn how to use different journal techniques to build structure in your journal. The Five-Minute Sprint, for instance, has time limits and boundaries. The Structured Write has clearly sequenced tasks. Sentence Stems have end limits.

Two other components to the anchor of structure are containment and pacing. Containment is like the safety net under circus acrobats. They're probably not going to need it, but why take chances?

When you write, you are moving thoughts, feelings and energy out of your mind and body and into a neutral, receptive place where they are stored safely. This can feel unboundaried and oceanic without some simple containment skills.

The easiest containment skill of all is to literally use your journal as a container. When you're finished, close the book and put it away. You can also maximize containment by using the page margins as boundaries. If necessary, draw borders on your page and keep your writing within them. Also give yourself time limits. Tell yourself you'll stop after fifteen minutes or two pages. The technique of Clustering (chapter 5) is a good technique for containment because it looks like a container.

Many people avoid writing about difficult or complex issues because they're concerned about getting in too deeply. What do you do with all the feelings that might come up? What happens when you're done writing and you have to go back to your life?

Pace yourself in your writing, just as you pace yourself during a run or a hike. Back off when you start feeling emotionally fatigued or stressed. Stop when you need to. It's unhealthy to ignore your own warning signs.

One good way to pace yourself is to move. Stand up and stretch. Get a drink of water. Then come back. The first few times you might lose your train of thought, but with practice you'll learn how to reenter your writing just where you left it.

When you know you're headed for some journal white water, plan your pacing in advance. Write messages to yourself in the margins of your empty pages: *Breathe. Drink water. Stretch. Move.* Stop where you are when you come across a message. Then come back.

Practice being a dolphin. Dive deeply and surface. Go into the heart of your writing, then come sharply to the surface, look around, grab some air, go back into it. Practice this when you don't need it so it will be familiar when you do.

## Reflection

The anchor of reflection helps you make sense of all the other anchors. This anchor weaves the thread of connection through your writing through feedback and review. It helps you find your patterns, cycles, themes, insights and awareness.

Develop the habit of instant replay. When you finish a journal entry, set it aside for a few minutes. Let it steep like a teabag. Then read it over and briefly answer these three questions:

- What do I notice?
- How do I feel?
- What do I do next?

You may want to write your replay statements in the margin, or at an angle across the page, so that you can find them easily. You can also use a highlighter.

The instant replay can also be used to reflect on an

event, conversation, transaction or meeting. Recap it in a Five-Minute Sprint (chapter 5), then stand back and assess. As you reviewed the situation, what did you focus on? What did you leave out? What's the next step to take?

Use the top and side page margins for miscellaneous jottings: phone numbers, things to remember, fleeting thoughts, items to get at the store. Circle or box these items so you can easily find them. This helps keep the flow of writing going while planting seeds of action steps. Michael offers another perspective:

> I've been experimenting with making no section or writing in the journal more important than any other. I used to scrunch in at the very top of the page in small letters notes to myself about things I wanted to remember for the future. Now I give them equal space.

Each volume of your journal is a chapter in the book of your life. Leave several pages at the end of every volume for a summary. Reread the entire book, preferably in one sitting. If you don't mind marking up your journal, use different-colored highlighters: Blue for action steps to take, yellow for feelings, green for new ideas, orange for dreams. If you don't want to mark up your journal, number the pages and keep an index on the inside back cover.

Some questions to ask yourself as you reflect:

- What were the themes of this volume?
- What has changed?
- What has remained the same?
- What have my lessons been?

- How have I grown?
- What have been the predominant feelings in this volume?
- What do I want to take with me into the next volume?
- How do I feel about the work I have done in this journal?

Not surprisingly, the eight anchors carry over into your life. In fact, your journal is an excellent place to try on any number of new behaviors that you're cultivating in life. Your journal becomes both a literal and a symbolic "self-object"—an external manifestation of who you are inside. So as you get healthier and more self-aware through your journal, other areas of your life start subtly shifting and rearranging. As you start giving yourself permission to write when and how you want, for instance, you might find yourself being less judgmental and restrictive in other areas. As you become more honest in your journal, you become more honest in your relationships. As you reflect on your progress, you notice you're moving ahead. As above, so below; as within, so without.

## Chapter Five

# THE JOURNAL TOOLBOX

*L*ike the toolbox in your garage or basement, the journal toolbox contains devices that help you reach into unfamiliar places, loosen worn-out beliefs or attitudes, connect seemingly disparate events or ideas and build new and different patterns for your life.

Some of the techniques in the journal toolbox may feel just as unfamiliar and awkward as a socket wrench does the first time you use it. Just as you eventually master a socket wrench, journal mastery comes with practice, patience and perseverance.

Don't expect to respond to every journal tool equally. As you are drawn to the various processes in this book, you'll likely discover a handful of writing techniques that consistently produce satisfying results. Others may not fit your style. This is normal.

## The Tools

Here is an alphabetical list of the journal tools you'll be working with in this book. The numbers indicate where each technique falls on the ten-rung journal ladder, which you'll learn about later in this chapter. For a more complete treatment of these techniques, please see my first book, *Journal to the Self*, and my workbook, *The Way of the Journal.* The Peer Dialogue technique was developed during this project and appears here in print for the first time.

*AlphaPoems (5).* A quick, easy and startlingly effective poetry device. Start by writing the alphabet (or a key word or phrase, or even a random selection of letters) vertically down your page. Then create a poem in which each line of the poem begins with the next successive letter. It's perfectly okay to make Xceptions for Xtra-hard letters. The structure of knowing where the next line starts seems to free up the imagination. AlphaPoems sound like something straight out of a fourth-grade classroom until you've tried one. Then you're hooked.

### AN ALPHAPOEM ON ALPHAPOEMS

Anticipate a
Blossoming of
Creative
Delight!
Effortless, really, once you
Find the rhythm and the pace.
Gather up the thoughts you hold secret in your
Heart.
Imagine them
Just drifting out, a

Kaleidoscope of
Letters
Making words.
No "rules" to follow (except the
Obvious one). Perhaps you'll find a
Poet inside?
Quite likely!
Reread your AlphaPoems; you'll find them
Startlingly
True—an
Unusual way to give
Voice to the
Wails, wonderings, whimpers, whys, wins.
Xhilarating feeling to find
You've reached the
Zenith of the poem!

*Artmaking (9).* So what if you can't draw? This is *your* journal! Giving form, shape and color to your thoughts and feelings is another way of communicating with yourself. As an alternative to drawing or painting, try collage, or mount a single picture cut from a magazine or newspaper and write about what it evokes in you.

Art is a visual metaphor that helps you communicate the context of your thought process. It offers distance and literally lets you look at your issue from a detached point of view. Art provides a bridge from the unknown to the known.

Art for its own sake is satisfying. If you want to process your artwork when you're done, start by giving your picture or collage a name. As you look at your picture, what do you notice? What are you aware of? Jot down your observations. How did you feel as you made the picture? How do you feel now as you look at it? What

in the picture most draws your attention? Do you notice
themes such as repeated shapes, colors, objects? How
does this picture seem to speak to your life as you are
living it today? How does the title relate to your issue?

If you want to move a layer deeper, enter into the
picture as you might a dream. Dialogue with the symbols
or people in the picture. Place yourself in the picture
somewhere and write about the imaginal experience of
being inside the picture. Climb into the picture and
"become" one of the forms or colors. Write from that perspective. Yes, you're making it up. Do it anyway.

*Captured Moments (5).* Vignettes capturing the sensations
of a particularly meaningful or emotional experience.
Captured Moments are sensual; pull out all the stops and
stretch for the most descriptive adjectives and verbs you
can find. A collection of Captured Moments becomes like
a written photo album, preserving memories for the
future.

Any experience that grips you with its intensity or
emotion is a good subject for a Captured Moment. Close
your eyes now and recall your own moments of exquisite
pleasure or pain: a brilliant coral sunset; the birth of a
baby; the death of a loved one; an experience of the
divine; a bruised or broken heart; an audience's
applause; the marathon's finish line. As you become
familiar with this journal device, you'll start to recognize
experiences as Captured Moments material. They're good
for containing painful experiences because they're brief—
usually just a few paragraphs—and very intense.

*Character Sketch (7).* A written portrait of another person
or a part of yourself. Writing about another—especially

someone you're in conflict with or admire greatly—is an excellent opportunity to tune in to your projections.

Begin by closing your eyes and imagining this person or part of yourself. What do you notice first? Physical qualities? Feelings? "Essence"? What are this person's likes and dislikes? What is important to him/her? How do you feel about this person? What does s/he need, want, fear? What do you and this person have as points of dis/agreement? What annoys or intimidates you about this person? What attracts you? What is this person's message? Try this as a Structured Write, Cluster or just as a List. Your Character Sketch may shift into a Dialogue.

The different parts of yourself—your subpersonalities—are also good candidates for Character Sketches. Who's your Inner Critic? Your Wounded Child? Your Warrior? Write descriptions of them as if they were people. Do the sketches actually describe people in your life? Your father/mother, boss, son/daughter, role model, someone with whom you have conflict?

You can come to know more about your feelings and emotions by imagining them as people or animals and writing Character Sketches about them. What does this emotion look like? Where does he/she/it hang out? What is it hungry for? When and how did you become acquainted? What does it ask of you?

Challenge is very large. He casts a great shadow, but he is light on his feet and can be quite exuberant, walking forward to welcome you with his hand extended and a wide grin on his face. His face clouds over, though, if you spend too much time discussing Doubt and Fear. He doesn't have much use for them and stopped sending them Christmas cards though he has a room and an office in town, and he travels a great deal. Everywhere he stays he has a lot of books on a wide variety of subjects. He is always hanging around with Curiosity and they have many interesting discussions. Being with Challenge is very intellectually stimulating and energizing, but sometimes I find it hard to keep my energy level up when he is not around. (Lesley)

*Clustering (4).* Also called mind-mapping or webbing, a Cluster is visual free association around a central word or phrase. Lines and circles connect key thoughts and associations to the central core. Clustering combines the intuitive aspects of free association with just enough structure to organize and make connections. It's an excellent technique for managing projects and generating creative flow. It's also good for gathering up the loose ends of the day: Try a Cluster with today's date as the central point. Include Best Thing/Worst Thing du Jour. Here's a Daily Cluster—the second entry in Taylor's journal:

*Community Journals (4).* Consider keeping an ongoing communication book with your spouse, roommate, lover or kids. Keep it in a neutral and accessible location. Use it as an ongoing forum for expression of opinion, emotion, point of view or negotiation. A community journal is an effective way to share your feelings with those closest to you.

*Dialogue (6).* A marvel of flexibility, the Dialogue technique is the Swiss Army knife of the journal toolbox. It's an imaginary conversation in which you write both parts. On the page, it looks like a movie or theater script.

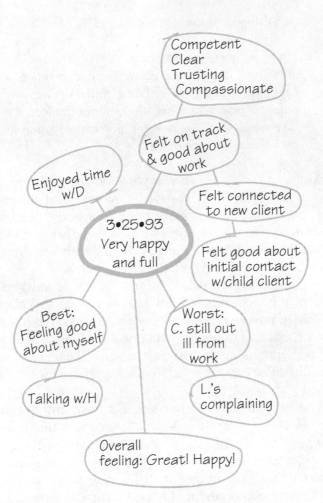

*This stringing together of the day feels comfortable and non-threatening. It feels like a good and simple beginning to my journaling experience. (Taylor)*

ME: Hi, Dialogue. Tell me about yourself.

D: I'm a written conversation with anyone or anything. I'm good for giving voice to intuition. I help with problem-solving and sorting out different points of view. I'm a shapechanger; I'll take on any role you want. Sometimes I unfold over hours, or even days.

You can dialogue with anyone or anything: people in your life, people in your past, yourself at different points in your life, parts of yourself, your body, blocks or resistances, feelings, possessions, values, dream characters or symbols, guides, Higher Power. You're limited only by your imagination!

Some tips for journal dialogue: Take it seriously; this is one of the most reliable devices for insight and clarity. It's entirely possible that it will seem as if you're making it up, or that the dialogue is taking on a life of its own. Both perceptions are completely normal. Dialogues tend to unfold in waves; respect the silence and don't rush yourself.

The ground rules: Either side may ask any question and receive an honest answer. Sometimes the honest answer is "I don't know" or "Pass." Likewise, either side may make any statement or express any opinion and be listened to without argument. It's a nice touch to thank your Dialogue partner at the end. Ask if you can talk again.

*Dream Journals (9; varies).* Your life becomes transparent when you start paying attention to what goes on in your unconscious moments. Writing down your dreams is the first step. Give your dream a name. From there you can crack the code many different ways. Fascinating! Chapter 14 is all about using your journal to work with dreams.

*Five-Minute Writing Sprint (2).* Who said journal writing takes a lot of time? Pick a subject, any subject: What's going on, the present moment, a person or relationship, your feeling or mood, a decision or choice, a check-in with yourself, the best/worst thing of the day, an insight or "aha," a to-do list, and so on. Set the kitchen timer or the beeper on your watch for five minutes. Write without stopping until time is up. Reread what you've written. Underline or mark with an asterisk in the margin anything you want to follow up or to pursue further. Continue if you want to and have time; come back to it later if you don't. The Five-Minute Sprint is useful when you have a lot going on, need clarity and focus, and/or have limited time and don't want to get absorbed in a long journal process.

If five minutes aren't enough, then do ten-minute sprints. Be sure to stop when you said you would. It's vitally important for two reasons: First, when the heat's cranked up, the bottom line rushes up to meet you. You can write in five minutes what it takes an hour to wander into. Second, you learn to trust yourself to do what you say you're going to do. This is crucial for times when you're working through difficult material.

*Free Writing (10).* This unstructured, unboundaried, free-form narrative writing starts anywhere and goes where it pleases. Although it is the fallback technique of nearly every journal writer, it isn't necessarily the most effective or efficient. Its inherent fluidity places it at the very top of the journal ladder.

Free writing is best done quickly and bravely. Plunge head-on into the writing and keep your pen to paper until you come to a natural shift. Be forewarned that unboundaried writing often releases emotion, and the swiftness and intensity may catch you off guard. If you need to, go ahead and slow down by setting the timer, getting up and stretching, quitting at the end of the page and/or shifting to a more structured writing process.

As a meditation, free writing invites you to ride the inky wave and dive into the "knowledge beyond understanding that comes to us at depth," as master journal teacher Ira Progoff states in his classic book *At a Journal Workshop.*

*Letters (7).* Writing is a powerful way to open doors to communication. Because letters are intentionally a one-way communication, they're a good choice when you have something to say and want to say it without interruption.

Unsent Letters, often used effectively to discharge strong emotion, are a way of being safely out of control. They are usually written with the specific intention that they will not be sent. Make a ceremony out of destroying your Unsent Letter when it has served its cathartic purpose. Let the burning or tearing of the paper symbolize the harmless release of the discharged feeling.

*Lists (3) and Lists of 100 (5).* Start thinking of your to-do lists as journal entries. Lists are pragmatic and efficient, and they can't be beat for gathering quick information.

A surefire way to clarify thoughts, identify patterns,

get below the surface, get past the obvious, and quickly gather data: Lists of 100. That's right—a hundred items. Repetition is an important part of the process. Just write the next thing in your mind, even if you've already written it lots of times. You can write in words and phrases to make the list go faster. Just get it down as quickly as possible. It takes about twenty to thirty minutes to write a hundred entries. When you're done, go back and find the themes. For instance, a list of "100 Current Crazymakers" yielded the cheerful news that forty-seven of my entries had to do with administrative paperwork—reports to write, stacks of filing, forms to fill out. I hate that stuff. After rereading my lists I cleared my calendar, unplugged the phone, devoted myself to desk taming, and enjoyed the disappearance of nearly half my stress.

In *Journal to the Self* there's a list of 100 Things to Write a List of 100 About. Try these, or make up your own:

100 Things I Need or Want to Do
100 Sources of Stress
100 Blessings I Forget to Count
100 Things That Piss Me Off
100 Outdated Beliefs
100 Ways I Hide
100 Secrets
100 Things to Accomplish in the Next Year
100 Things I've Never Mourned
100 Feelings I'm Having
100 Qualities to Develop
100 Things to Forgive Myself For

*Inner Wisdom (9).* "Man does indeed know intuitively

more than he rationally understands," continues Ira Progoff. Access a quiet state through relaxation or deep breathing and request guidance from the part of you that knows your truth. The Dialogue technique is helpful. Write whatever comes, or write a letter to yourself from your inner guidance. Try a free-writing meditation; or just jot down images or notes.

To blast through creative blocks, invoke the Muse. For twelve-step recovery work, ask your Higher Power to be present. Imagine the presence of departed loved ones, guides or angels. Gaze upon the image of Christ, a saint, a biblical figure, a master teacher, a holy man or woman. Let your writing come from a place deep within. Writing from your inner wisdom involves temporarily suspending normal states of rational consciousness. Thus, it is common and normal to find yourself writing things that sound more profound, poetic or wise than you'd think yourself capable of writing. No matter how foreign and odd your answers and insights might seem at first, try to trust them.

*Peer Dialogue (7).* A conflict-resolution dialogue in which you, in imagery, create a relationship of equals by adjusting the power dynamics between you and your dialogue partner. With a level playing field, free of the top dog/underdog dynamics of real life, you can create parity long enough to communicate as equals.

This is done by freely granting either party to the dialogue whatever is needed to effectively communicate. For starters, it's helpful to equalize the age relationship so that you and your dialogue partner are peers. Do this through mental imagery.

For instance, if you're dialoguing with a parent who

was abusive to you as a child, imagine yourself at an age when you were abused. How old was your parent then? Imagine your parent at that age, and grow yourself up to your present age. You should be at least in the same generation, and perhaps quite close in age.

Conversely, you can "youthen" the older partner. To work with your ten-year-old son in Peer Dialogue, for instance, you may want to imagine yourself when you were ten and reconnect with the emotions, struggles and yearnings of that time in your life.

Continue to alter one or both partners until they have equal footing. Then, from the perspective of a peer, write a Character Sketch of your dialogue partner. Next, attribute qualities to either side that will help with effective conflict management. For example, an angry person might need words instead of violent actions; a hesitant person might need empowerment; a confused person might need clarity.

Finally, with a clear intention to respect each partner, begin the dialogue. Two effective places to close are when you come to resolution, or when you come to awareness that you are not yet ready to come to resolution. You can always come back to the dialogue another time.

*Perspectives (8).* An alteration in point of view that provides a different perspective on an event or situation. Propel yourself backward or forward in time and write as if it were the past or the future. For instance, One Year from Today entries offer glimpses into what you might be holding as secret desires or unvoiced concerns. When you're having trouble with decision-making, try jumping ahead to the other side of the decision and writing as if you had already made the choice. You might be surprised by what you "decide"!

An entry written from the perspective of someone else lets you stroll around to another point on the circle of truth and check out the view. It lets you step into another's skin long enough to sense what might be motivating him/her. The compassion inherent in this perspective eases the way to understanding and healing.

*Poetry (9).* President Clinton's request that Maya Angelou write and present his inaugural poem spotlighted the renaissance of this evocative, provocative, invocative literary form. In cities on both American coasts poetry "slams" reminiscent of the beatnik coffee houses of the 1950s are making a 1990s comeback; as I write this chapter, MTV features the first of its spoken-word "Unplugged" concerts with several youthful poets performing to an enthusiastic crowd.

Certain aspects of your healing journey won't respond well to analytic, task-oriented approaches. If there's something going on that you can't quite grasp rationally, turn to the poetic for help. Notable for its ability to simultaneously reveal and conceal, poetry is especially helpful when you are viscerally called to reach deep inside yourself.

In her excellent book *Shrapnel in the Heart: Letters and Remembrances From the Vietnam Veterans Memorial,* journalist Laura Palmer notes the quantity and richness of poetry left at the wall.

> I wondered why people who may have had little exposure to poetry chose it as a way to express their feelings. The best explanation for this phenomenon

came from a Vietnam vet in Wichita, Kansas, Rich Rogers, who told me, "When you've been to the abyss and stared into the pit of hell, you look for the opposite to explain it, sort of like yin and yang."

If poetry is unfamiliar to you, learn from the master teachers. Surround yourself with the works of classic and contemporary poets such as Marge Piercy, Walt Whitman, Edna St. Vincent Millay, Robert Frost, Emily Dickinson, Rainer Maria Rilke, Maya Angelou, Robert Bly, Linda Pastan, David Whyte, James Kavanaugh, Wendell Berry and Judith Viorst. Start at the public library. You may want to respond to others' poems with your own reflective prose, or you may want to try your hand at capturing the absolute essence of a thought in the stiletto sharpness of poetic image.

*Questions (see Springboards).*

*Sentence Stems (1).* It doesn't get any quicker or easier than this. Give yourself the first word or phrase of a sentence (*I feel*—or *Today I want to accomplish*—) and finish the thought one or a dozen different ways. Capitalize on the free-associative qualities of Sentence Stems by not censoring or editing your writing.

*Springboards (8).* A topic sentence or question written at the beginning of a journal entry; it helps focus and clarify the writing. As a general rule, Springboards written as statements or Sentence Stems tend to stimulate thoughts and opinions; Springboards written as questions tend to stimulate feelings and beliefs.

Questions also springboard you into philosophical

musings and self-examination. "Be patient toward all that is unsolved in your heart," wrote the poet Rilke. "Try to love the questions themselves like locked rooms and like books that are written in a foreign tongue." Everything you need to know is contained in the questions you ask. As a journal device, Springboards will keep you going for pages, hours, days—even for life.

*Structured Write (3).* A methodical and efficient way to explore precipitants, current realities, emotions and desired outcomes of an issue. Structured Writes are a series of Springboard statements or questions chained sequentially to provide an orderly flow of information. Keep your responses to each question or stem brief; one or two sentences are plenty. The entire process shouldn't take more than ten or fifteen minutes. From this overview you'll then be able to pinpoint ideas or beliefs to explore more thoroughly. A basic Structured Write goes something like this:

- I want to explore . . .
- The first thing that comes to mind is . . .
- Beneath the surface I find . . .
- What feels uncomfortable or disturbs me about this is . . .
- What excites or inspires me about this is . . .
- I would benefit from . . .
- My next step is . . .

## The Journal Ladder

The journal ladder is a development continuum that starts with the most highly structured, highly contained, highly paced journal technique (Sentence Stems) and gradually builds in fluidity, openness and insight. It ends at the place where most people begin—Free Writing.

In my work as a clinical journal therapist I am constantly surprised at the number of people who write journals even though it's painful, unsatisfying, frustrating, intimidating or otherwise difficult. In fact, a two-year study I conducted at a treatment center for post-traumatic stress disorder indicated that fully 96 percent of the research subjects experienced significant obstacles, blocks or barriers to satisfying journalkeeping!

"The discomfort was so high," I wrote in *The Way of the Journal,* "that many clients perceived the journal as a sort of psychoid cod liver oil: The cure was worse than what ailed 'em."

The obstacles fell into a few major categories. The first was a reluctance to see before them the reality of their lives. "If I write, I see how painful my life really is," was a common response. "I sometimes find out things I didn't want to know."

The second set of obstacles related to the journal itself. Frustrations with getting started, staying motivated, managing a stop/start writing pattern and getting beyond fluff presented blocks or barriers for many. Some reported self-consciousness about their level of skill in writing or using language, and others noted the paralysis of perfectionism.

Several other reasons for diary block could be lumped together under the general category of self-management. These included struggles with the Inner Critic or Inner Censor; difficulty finding enough time for effective writing; feeling worse instead of better after a journal session. Also in this category was a phenomenon that I called the paper trail syndrome. A typical comment went something like, "Are you nuts? If I'm not even supposed to talk about my family secrets or show that I have feelings, why on earth would I write that stuff down?"

I asked my clients what would make journal writing easier. They clamored for education and skills to help them use the journal as a tool for growth and recovery. They wanted to learn different ways to write that would move them beyond the same old stuff. "I've been recycling my garbage for years," one client said. "Now I want to learn how to compost it!"

Clients also asked for practical, concrete ideas on how to develop and maintain a relationship with their journals. They wanted to learn how to read their own minds. They wanted to turn to their journals as they would to trusted friends. Consistency, structure, balance and safety were important to them.

When I looked at how the clients were utilizing their journals, it became clear why they were experiencing difficulties. I found that in the absence of a better idea, just about everyone sat down with a blank page or computer screen and blasted away—or tried to.

No wonder they were in trouble. Free Writing, you will recall, is unboundaried, unstructured and nondirected. It starts anywhere at all and usually goes off in unanticipated directions.

When it is used purposefully and intentionally, Free Writing can be a highly effective technique that offers clarity, insight and intuitive connection. But as a default technique, it can feel uncontrolled and risky, like a colt without a bridle or a free-fall with an unreliable parachute. At other times it can feel like a dog leashed to a clothesline, going nowhere in tight, unsatisfying circles.

It occurred to me that the solution might be quite simple. If unstructured, unpaced, uncontained writing was not a good starting place, then maybe structured, paced, contained writing would work better. Thus was born the journal ladder (see page 75), a developmental approach that starts with maximum structure, pacing and containment and gradually moves toward insight, fluidity and openness. Balance and permission are built in at every stage. The continuum ends with free writing, where most people begin.

With the foundation of structure anchoring your journal, you can learn to match your mood, issue or desired outcome with a journal intervention that enhances your likelihood of success. You'll learn, for instance, that highly charged emotional states or feelings of pressure are served by techniques that maximize containment, such as Clustering or Five-Minute Sprints. You'll learn that external or internal disorganization and chaos are calmed with the structure of Sentence Stems or AlphaPoems. You'll learn that you can retrieve information efficiently with a Structured Write. You'll also learn that when you want access to inner wisdom, you can go up the ladder to the more insight-oriented techniques, like Dialogue, Springboards and, yes, Free Writing.

There are some twenty techniques on the journal ladder. Each carries a numerical ranking between one and ten. The lower numbers represent ways to write that are well structured, concrete, practical and immediately useful. As you move up the ladder, the techniques become increasingly more abstract, insightful, intuitive.

The midrange is good for uncovering patterns and connections; in the upper range, you can connect with inner
guidance and creativity.

With a little practice, you can teach yourself to
approach your life issues with journal techniques that
predict successful outcomes. You just can't know how
liberating this is until you've experienced it.

## The Journal Toolbox

Your journal toolbox is now equipped. The tools won't
rust or break down. They're renewable; they get
stronger and sharper with use. Now and then, lightly
oil the less-used tools with your attention. Like the
toolbox that fascinated Christian at the Smithsonian
Institute, your journal tools will take on the essence of
your life.

The piano maker's toolbox . . . was the most
interesting and elaborate—a jewel, a sculptural
object in its own right. There were 700 or so tools
packed into an intricately made inlaid wooden chest,
screwdrivers, pliers, rasps, wrenches, hammers, drills,
awls, saws, all set in layer upon layer only six inches
or so deep, with the freemason's compass insignia—
but the compass was not flat, it was real and could be
utilized for measuring. All the tools were themselves
hand-made. It took so long to decipher it. I spent
almost an hour with it, mesmerized, read it like a
book, stood entranced. . . . I felt the essence of the
person who made it. Here was this person's spirit in a

# THE JOURNAL LADDER

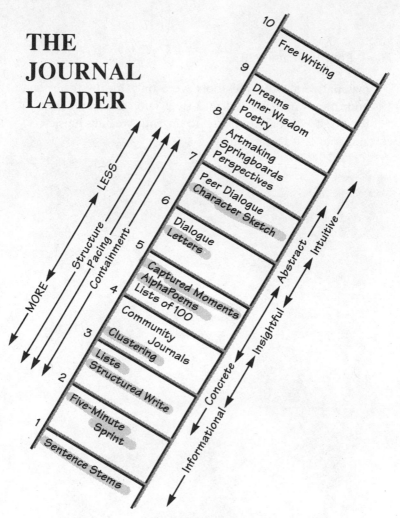

- 10 Free Writing
- 9 Dreams / Inner Wisdom / Poetry
- 8 Artmaking / Springboards / Perspectives
- 7 Peer Dialogue / Character Sketch
- 6 Dialogue / Letters
- 5 Captured Moments / AlphaPoems / Lists of 100
- 4 Community / Journals
- 3 Clustering
- 2 Lists / Structured Write
- 1 Five-Minute Sprint / Sentence Stems

MORE — LESS

Structure — Pacing — Containment

Informational — Concrete — Insightful — Intuitive — Abstract

| | |
|---|---|
| Structure: | Foundation, form, sequenced tasks, orderliness |
| Pacing: | Rhythm, movement, timing |
| Containment: | Boundaries, limits |
| Concrete: | Easy to grasp or implement, realistic |
| Abstract: | Symbolic, metaphoric, multidimensional |
| Informational: | Practical, immediately useful |
| Insightful: | Connections, patterns, awarenesses |
| Intuitive: | "Aha" experience, sudden knowing, internal wisdom |

*(Note: Techniques that are shaded can be completed in 5–15 minutes.)*

material form. And the tools were only means to an end, transforming wood and steel into an instrument that itself was only a means to an end, creating music and sound. It was a miracle.

*Chapter Six*

# HEALING THE WOUNDED WRITER

*I*f you have ever been criticized, humiliated, taunted or punished because of what you wrote or how you wrote it, there's a good chance you've got writing wounds.

You're far from alone. In the attics of the psyche, most people have a few dusty trunks filled with writing wounds—traumas large and small associated with writing.

In childhood, these often take the form of seemingly innocuous teachings and redirections. Culturally, for instance, we have a distinct preference for right-handedness. In *The Power of the Other Hand*, art therapist Lucia Capacchione quotes Benjamin Franklin's petition to the Superintendents of Education. It is signed THE LEFT HAND:

> From my infancy I have been led to consider my sister
> as a being of more educated rank. I was suffered to

grow up without the least instruction, while nothing
was spared in her education. She had masters to teach
her writing, drawing, music and other accom-
plishments, but if by chance I touched a pencil, a pen,
or a needle I was bitterly rebuked; and more than
once I have been beaten for being awkward and
wanting a graceful manner.

Capacchione's work with handedness has revealed a
group of people she calls switch-overs, left-handers who
were forced by parents or teachers to write with their
right hands:

My clinical experience confirms that much psychological damage was done. Often these individuals
would have trouble finding my office for their first art
therapy session. In private work it would frequently be
revealed that they had great difficulty finding their way
in life. They chose the "wrong" careers, seemed to be
living in unsatisfying relationships and locations.
Something very basic had been betrayed at an early
age, and it appeared to have long-term effects.

A surprising number of men avoid writing because
they are self-conscious about the appearance they project
through their penmanship.

I just don't like the way my writing looks on the
page. It's sloppy and hard to read. My staff
harasses me about it all the time. So I dictate into a
tape recorder and let my secretary figure it out. If I'm
going to look bad in writing, then I can't afford to do
it. (William)

When the wounding relates specifically to reflective writing, it is felt even more deeply.

Last summer I was involved in a supervisory qualification program at work. All candidates were asked to keep a journal of issues, insights and concerns. I promised myself I'd write a *real* journal and be open and honest, even though it would be handed in. My supervisor's feedback was devastating. He called me a wimp and made other unwelcome comments and suggestions. I was hurt, flabbergasted and stunned. Then I got angry. My journals from that point on were coded and guarded. My true journaling was pushed underground. (Jim)

When trauma associated with writing is layered on top of physical or emotional childhood trauma, the results can be devastating. As the journal therapist for a clientele of adults who were badly abused as children, I heard many stories of children raised in violent families who attempted to bypass the "don't tell/don't feel" directives by unloading in writing. The trauma associated with eventual discovery of their diaries or journals was often catastrophic. Like Capacchione's, my clinical experience confirms that much psychological damage was done, and it contributed to long-term damaging effects on the capacities for trust and self-disclosure.

Without question the most common trauma happens sometime in the middle-school years, when we learned editing skills such as grammar, punctuation, sentence structure and composition. You should see the flood of relief when I suggest that writing and editing are two separate functions, that in the journal there's no reason to edit unless you want to. There's also plenty of trauma associated with feeling embarrassed or ashamed at supposed deficiencies in creativity or imagination.

Trauma connected with writing, however serious or inconsequential it may appear, almost always interferes with the ability to write with depth, spontaneity, authority and confidence. That's the bad news. The good news: Wounded writers can heal.

## PICK UP YOUR PEN

The way to heal writing wounds is to write. If you can't write, try this six-step process. It takes about an hour; do it in one sitting. I'll first list the six steps, and then we'll go through them. The examples came from Daniel:

1. **Identify** your wounds.
2. **Note** themes and patterns.
3. **Explore** one incident.
4. **Reclaim** your writing.
5. **Synthesize** the learning.
6. **Acknowledge** yourself.

### Identify Your Wounds

Divide your page vertically down the middle. On the left side, make a list of memories, images and recollections of incidents in which you remember feeling hurt, humiliated, punished or rejected because of what you wrote or how you wrote it. Write this list in

| Memories/Images/ Recollections | Messages Received |
|---|---|
| **1.** Being made fun of because I am left-handed | **1.** Someone who is left-handed isn't worth much and doesn't fit into a "normal" world. |
| **2.** Being made to write on a blackboard as punishment | **2.** I can't even write well on a desk, much less a wall not made for lefties. I hate this! |
| **3.** Being told that my writing wasn't readable | **3.** I can't write, so why try? |
| **4.** Being told I need to proof my memos better | **4.** I don't make the time; therefore I shouldn't bother. |
| **5.** Having my writing made fun of | **5.** Embarrassed; lack of self-esteem; my self-worth is tied up in how well I write. |
| **6.** Told to print rather than write so it could be read | **6.** What makes anyone think my printing is any better? |
| **7.** Fear of being judged by the way my writing looks | **7.** I won't be accepted and I might be rejected. |
| **8.** My mom telling me she can't read my writing | **8.** My mom wants a son who can write—she might not love me as much if she can't read it. |
| **9.** My secretary asking me what words are that she can't read | **9.** You jerk, it continues; you need to learn to write! |

simple phrases. Leave yourself a couple of lines between items.

Opposite each incident, on the right side, note the messages you received or told yourself. These messages may have related to yourself, your writing, the person criticizing you or life itself. Don't spend too much time trying to figure out the messages. If you really don't know, then write down the messages that you might have told yourself. Your first impressions will do just fine.

## Note Themes and Patterns

Review your list. Do you notice any themes or patterns? Note them.

I want to write. I can't write. I worry too much about my writing and how it looks. It gets in the way of my content and expression.

## Explore One Incident

Choose an incident from your list, or choose one of your themes or patterns. Explore it in a Five-Minute Sprint.

My fiancée said to me, "Let me address our wedding invitations. I want people to be able to read them." She said it in a kidding way and wasn't attacking, but here was the person I love and am going to marry. I want to please her, and she's telling me I can't write well.

This isn't the first time she has mentioned it to me.

Each time she does, it isn't so much what she says as all the old messages it brings up. I feel like a failure. I feel like I'm not worthy because people can't read my writing. So why do I even try?

## Reclaim Your Writing

Write an Unsent Letter expressing your anger, hurt, frustration, shame or other feelings. The letter could be written to one specific person, or it might be more generalized. In this letter, reclaim your writing.

Dear Everyone: I can write. I am a writer. I am telling all of your old messages from the past to get the hell out of my life. I am sick and tired of you telling me that I can't write, you can't read it, I should print, I should type it. Well, you know what? I have news for you. I can write. Maybe it doesn't look the way you think it should, but my ability to write isn't tied up in how elegant it looks on paper. I have made excuses all my life as to why I can't write: I'm left-handed, I don't have the right paper or pen, I don't have enough time. These excuses worked for years but they aren't working any more. I'm 45 years old. This is it. This is what you get, and it's either acceptable or it's not. It doesn't mean I'm not a worthy person or that I can't write. It simply means my style of writing is unique and me. I am me. I am free.

As an alternative, you can write an Unsent Letter to yourself from someone who criticized or hurt you. In the letter, let this person apologize to you and offer amends for the wounding.

## Synthesize the Learning

So, how was it? Review what you've written, and in a few sentences, reflect on the process. What did you learn? What's shifted for you? Where do you go from here?

> This was an enlightening experience. I was able to separate on paper and in my mind that my *writing* and my *handwriting* are not one and the same. I knew this in my head, but I don't think it had ever broken through to my actual belief system. This writing exercise reinforced what I knew but maybe didn't totally believe.

## Acknowledge Yourself

Thank yourself for doing this work.

> Good job, Daniel, now believe it and move onward with your writing—write, write, write!

As page after page of Daniel's process rolled through my fax machine, I was profoundly moved by two things. First was the depth of his wounding. Second was the legibility of his writing. His penmanship is distinctive, with a pronounced slant and strong letters. He writes on every other line, so his long ascenders and descenders don't bump into one another. Daniel doesn't have the kind of writing you can take in at a glance, but neither is it impossible to read.

## Put Down Your Swords

Writing wounds are insidious. They often cause the paralysis that masquerades as "not enough time" or "not enough discipline" or "not getting around to it."

This process can help you move through much of your stuckness. When your writing wounds sneak back in like dandelions—and they will—stop and remind yourself of your new awarenesses. Reframe your old messages. Release them. And go write.

*Chapter Seven*

# THOSE LITTLE
# LOCKING DIARIES

*I*n a society sadly lacking in initiation rites for boys and girls alike, the adolescent diary is a significant female marker. When asked the question, How do you recall your first awareness of journals and diaries? men frequently respond with stories of these secretive little books.

I grew up with three older sisters. My first diary recollection is being six and having my oldest sister, then thirteen, yell at me for playing too loud with my trucks while she tried to write in her diary. When I was nine, my twin sisters were twelve. They always excluded me anyway, but when they got matching diaries I might as well not have existed. The thing that hurt the most was that even though they *said* their diaries were for really private stuff, all three shared them with each other. When I was ten I broke into one of the diaries and read it. I got punished worse for that than I did for shoplifting matchbox cars at Kmart. It wasn't even any good. (Mark)

Other men expressed admiration and mild envy at the diarykeeping ritual and offered ideas about the male counterpart.

> I always thought it was neat that girls were able to have those locked diaries. I wanted one too, but not bad enough to risk being made fun of by the other kids. (Edward)

> Maybe my baseball cards filled the same purpose. Playing with baseball cards and trading them with other kids let me dream about my future. (Mark)

My aunt gave me a diary the Christmas I was ten. I carry on that family tradition with my nieces and nephew. Last Christmas, however, I was unable to find a suitable diary for my nephew, Jake. Except for staid faux-leather covers with gilt-edged pages and gold script lettering, the cover designs were clearly tipped toward girl users. Even the "androgynous" designs such as clowns or cartoon animals had feminine touches: pink telephones, a hint of lace, a ribbon tying a shoe. This absence of suitable materials for boy diarists does not go unnoticed by men.

> Why was I as man-child socialized and yes, *conditioned* to believe that when girls/women decide it's time to have an interior life there is merchandise to support that? Where are the little locking books for boys? What do I offer my son? Even if there were a diary for an 11-year-old boy, what do I tell him to do with it? (Harold)

Some boys bucked tradition and wrote in diaries anyway, but the imperative for secrecy prevailed.

> I first started keeping a journal when I was in seventh or eighth grade. I bought a blank steno pad and a new blue pen. I locked them away in a box and hid the box in my closet. I can remember lying on my bed trying to invent some way that the locked box would explode or release acid to destroy the journal if someone tried to force their way into the box. I never did come up with anything that seemed workable, so I just hid the box deeper in my closet. I wrote in that pad every day until it was filled, and I have kept a journal in some form ever since. (John)

Throughout most of the stories was woven a common thread.

> I think my sister's diary was the first time I bought the message that girls are supported in having an emotional, interior, reflective life—and boys are not. As I write that, I realize I feel sad, jealous, resentful, ripped off. (Harold)

A recent journal conference featured community meals with open-mike journal readings. Anybody who wanted could share his or her writings. A young woman read excerpts from her first diary, written when she was eleven and twelve years old. Virtually every woman in the room found it hilariously funny. We were screaming, howling, stomping, slapping backs, pounding tables, gasping for breath. The man sitting next to me was baffled. "This is the diary of Everywoman," I explained. "All our first diaries sounded exactly like this." His expression registered doubt. "You mean . . . ?" he asked. I nodded. He rolled his eyes.

Yup. Our prepubescent battles of the sexes were

fought over such breathless prose as "Went to school, wore red pleated skirt, came home, did homework, ate dinner, washed dishes, listened to the radio, washed my hair." Or "Mark W. is SO CUTE!!!! I like him SO MUCH!!!! I'LL JUST DIE if he doesn't like me too!!!! I asked Sue to ask Steve to ask Mark if he liked me!!!!"

Content notwithstanding, the point remains that while most of us were growing up, little locking diaries were a province of girl children, just as Little League baseball was a province of boy children. Times have changed; this summer my nieces played on an otherwise all-boy Little League team, and I finally found a suitable diary for my nephew, Jake.

It has surprised me to find that several men I know are longtime journal writers. Journal writing is supported by women because they seek the support. Men would receive the same support if they sought it. . . . There's never been gender-specific books or classes for men on journaling. It's time. This book is a good start. (Mark)

In the social hour preceding my dinner address to the Toronto Women's Press Club, I found my attention drawn to an elegant woman of regal bearing who appeared to be in her seventies. She carried a small leather-bound book. By design or fate, I found myself seated next to her at dinner. Although her book was clearly aged, it was identical in shape and size to my first diary in 1961, my sister's first diary in 1971, my friend's daughter's first diary in 1981 and my niece's first diary in 1991. Even the familiar tiny clasp could have been unlocked with four decades of diary keys—or, for that matter, with any handy paper clip or bobby pin.

My dinner companion quickly turned the conversation around to the object of my curiosity.

"Since we're talking about diaries tonight," she said, "I thought I'd bring my first one. This is my one-year diary from 1935, when I was sixteen years old. I've kept one every year since."

I did some quick mental arithmetic. "Do you mean you have fifty-six volumes of one-year diaries?" I was staggered. In the archaeology of journals, this was a major dig.

A smile played gently on her lips. Her eyes softened. As I watched, a half century fell away, and I sat next to the sixteen-year-old girl, filled with promise and dreams, who inked her way through the year 1935 one day at a time.

"Yes," she said softly. "But this one is my favorite."

## PICK UP YOUR PEN

- Those little locking books are like small friends. It takes about five minutes to fill the daily page with a summary of your thoughts, feelings and activities. Stationery stores usually stock a few with adult unisex covers. It's a great way to start the journal habit.
- What was your first awareness of diaries or journals? What messages did you receive? How have those messages influenced your attitudes toward journals today?
- Sentence Stems:
  - The male children in my life who might benefit from a diary are—.
  - I could help them get started by—.
- Write about your first diary or journal. If this is your first, write about how it's going so far.

*Part Two*

# LAY DOWN
# YOUR SWORD

## Chapter Eight

# AUTHENTICITY

The room was silent save for the faint hum of the heating system and the determined scratching of pens on notebooks. The group was noting observations made in a guided imagery process. *Imagine yourself doing something you really enjoy. Now imagine that a private detective watches you do it. Write the detective's observations.*

Midway through the writing time, Jerry drew a sharp breath and closed his notebook. He glanced over at me, and I saw that his eyes were filled with pain. He seemed to shrink inside his crisp white button-down shirt.

When the group finished writing, I turned to Jerry. "Anything you want to share?" I asked.

*"This is fraudulent!"* His voice shook with an ancient, tired bitterness. "I am nothing but a fraud!" And he read:

The image is of a "father figure" with all the correct yuppie attributes. The image is just that, an image. There is a distinct absence of BEING—in particular, being present to the joy at depth of a profound relationship with my daughter. . . . Who or what is the image being? What motivates the image to appear or be recognized? What conspiracies influence its identity? It would seem that most of them have very little to do with BEING a father and much more to do with BEING CONSTRUED as a father. What's authentic about this? Well, it seems to be an authentic polarity.

"And what's fraudulent about this," he continued, "is that what I write is nothing like what I feel!"

The discrepancy between image/being, external/internal, acculturated self/authentic self—"the maintenance of the lie"—reverberates in the journals of men like an echo bouncing off canyon walls. The search for authenticity is a modern-day grail quest. It is the beating heart of many men's writings.

In my office hangs a small mirror. To introduce the concept of authenticity, I ask the members of the group to look at themselves in the mirror and write down what they notice. This process is usually punctuated with some self-conscious joking as the group members wait in single-file line and then make faces, practice smiling and reluctantly meet their own eyes in the mirror. The writings are poignant and telling:

I'm getting older, but I still look good. I like my looks. I've matured. Maybe I also like how I am inside.

Gray hair, thinning, "giant economy size" forehead. At least I didn't break the mirror! Good thing I couldn't see my paunch!

This was harder than it sounded. I can barely look myself in the eye. What do I think I'll see? Reminds me of that poem about facing the man in the mirror each day. Spooky.

The mirror on my office wall reflects the outer man. The journal, as mirror of the psyche, captures the inner man. Stay with the journal process for even a little while and you'll start to see the layers of your life. You'll begin to hear the voices inside. Like the increasingly soft leaves in each layer of an artichoke, the journal peels off layers of conditioning, habits and worn-out beliefs and reveals the heart nestled snugly inside.

What is authenticity? The men speak:

Authenticity is . . .
. . . being real.
. . . the *real* me. Not the one I show most of the time.
. . . something I can't sustain for long.
. . . honesty.
. . . when who I am on the outside matches who I am on the inside.
. . . genuine.
. . . living instead of being a robot.
. . . the real McCoy, natural, no bullshit.

My authentic self . . .
. . . is hidden.
. . . is warm, loving, affectionate.

. . . wants to get out of "jail."

. . . ?? I don't know my authentic self.

. . . tells the truth even when I don't want to know it.

. . . hates my job.

. . . is my Inner Child.

. . . is mad at me.

There is a scene in Disney's *Beauty and the Beast* in which the Beast, hunched over a desk, appears to be reflecting. We can't quite see what he's doing at the desk, but I like to think he's writing in a journal with a quill pen. The Beast, as you'll recall, didn't start out that way. His authentic self was trapped inside a beastly countenance because of something foolish he'd done as a youth. As punishment, he was made to live out his life with only one dimension of himself—his beastliness—in focus.

Sound familiar? It did to Greg. Greg is middle-aged. He has a modest white-collar job in a professional environment. He's been married to Gwendolyn for six years. They have no children. Greg goes to church, volunteers for his favorite charity and works on his own car. He and Gwendolyn invite friends over for dinner and cards on Friday nights. Like the outer Beast, the part of Greg the world sees is far from all of the story. He lives with a secret that he cannot share. He is gay.

Greg lives in a midsized city in the Bible Belt, where tolerance is limited, conformity is an equalizer and authenticity is a harsh master.

I am assaulted daily by anti-gay rhetoric on building walls, bathroom stalls and the media. The newspapers and police hound gay and lesbian people regularly in this city. As a result, the gay/lesbian community is really uptight. Crimes against gays, as well as racially motivated crimes, continue to rise.

Greg loves his wife, grieves over his life and grasps for meaning and purpose.

Sunday was full of angst! I cried on the way home from church. I had an overwhelming sense of loss come over me. Great sadness welled up inside me. It had to do with the impermanence of life—its transitory nature—and the loss of love.

I thought about my own mortality. I wondered how many years I had left. I counted up my Christmases. I thought about losing Gwendolyn through death or accident or divorce and what a devastating loss that would be. She's a hard person to reach—cold and aloof—my biggest challenge. But as Professor Henry Higgins says, I've grown accustomed to her face.

He mounts a daily battle against the challenge of being a homosexual man in a monogamous heterosexual marriage.

Gwendolyn and I both married late. We spent the first year negotiating territory. We knew our weak spots, but we hadn't yet lived them. Although Gwen was aware of my sexuality from the outset, neither one of us was prepared to deal with it, as it presented itself in marriage. We didn't know how to argue; we both came from abusive families. Our lives were miserable. I was miserable.

Although his marriage has now lasted six years and he no longer perceives his life or himself as miserable, suppression exacts a heavy toll.

> How do I function responsibly as a gay married man? This causes me problems. I am not sexually active outside of my marriage. I eat (compulsively) about this one.

Greg "stuffs" his feelings quite literally. He eats. A lifetime of food addiction and radical weight gains and losses has taken its toll; Greg's diabetes threatens his health. Early in his marriage, he checked himself into a residential eating disorder program. It was here that he first began using a journal in a purposeful way.

> I spent a month at a recovery center where daily journaling was used. Several months later, a dietician suggested I keep a journal of feelings associated with my eating habits. I generally "eat" my stress and anger. Journaling helps me to clear those feelings out of my head so I don't carry them around and feed them.

In addition to stress and anger, Greg also "swallows whole" many glimpses of his unmasked self. He fears that his thoughts and feelings might render him unacceptable to others.

> Something not many people know about me is . . . I deal with rampant sexual drives. . . . I worry about animals, poor people and the state of the earth. . . . I have periods of deep depression. . . . I want to go somewhere to learn something freeing that will put me

in touch with the playful child that lives in me. . . . I am fascinated with pornography. . . . I cry at movies, books and human suffering.

His authentic self gets breathing room in respites with a friend.

> I have one gay male friend who is currently in a relationship with a man. We get together once a week for lunch and air our grievances about our partners. I feel really alive when I'm with him. We often laugh at ourselves because we've discovered that relationship problems are relationship problems, regardless of gender or combination. He was previously married to a woman and has several grown children, so he can relate to my feelings.

His other outlet for his authentic self is his journal.

> I like journal writing. It has become a real friend to me. I generally write about angry or sexual feelings, problems at work, trouble I'm having with my wife, when I'm entertaining a particular sexual fantasy that would best be committed to paper than to action. Dreams when I remember them. What I want from my journal is a place where I can express my deepest, innermost feelings without being laughed at or judged or arrested. I want a place to go when I want self-pity, where I get to be right and justified in my actions no matter how infantile or self-serving. I write to unload inappropriate feelings (my definition!), to think things over, catalog events, argue with my wife, wrestle with my sexuality.

In therapy and in his journal, Greg has come to accept himself. Although he cannot change his sexual orientation and doesn't feel he can come out about it in public, he no longer feels as if he lives a lie. He does not deny or avoid his own truth, even if he chooses not to share it. For the most part, he is at peace.

I have tried hard to be a moral and ethical man—a man of my word who fights for issues of peace and justice. I try to be a good teacher and a good husband. I get the feeling sometimes that I haven't changed the world for the better, that I am a very small fish in a very big sea, that the bad guys still outnumber the good guys and that life just never will be fair. Other times I know I've made a difference. If I had my life to live over again I would travel more and be less afraid. I guess it's not too late.

## PICK UP YOUR PEN

These ideas progress along the journal ladder. It isn't necessary to do them in order, but if you're having difficulty, the earlier ones have a more built-in structure.

- Complete these Sentence Stems:
    Authenticity is . . .
    My authentic self . . .
    I am . . .
    I am not . . .
- Imagine that a newspaper or magazine reporter is interviewing you for a story. The questions: What habit would you most like to break? How did you meet your

best friend? Which one year of your life would you live over, and why? What do you consider your best attribute or feature? If you won a lottery that allowed you a comfortable lifestyle, how would you spend your time?

- Something very few people know about me . . .
- As children, we were natural, instinctive, intuitive and authentic. Children adapt to their environments by layering over the authentic self, but it is and always has been there. Look back at your childhood joys and pleasures. What do you remember? Jot down words or phrases.
- Cluster "authenticity" or "my authentic self."
- Discovering the authentic self involves unraveling layers of the conditioned or acculturated self. Try a List of 100 on one of these topics. When you're finished, go through and break the list into categories.
  - •100 Roles I Play
  - •100 Ways I Fake It
  - •100 Beliefs I Am Challenging
  - •100 Fears I Have about Being More Authentic
  - •100 Payoffs for Not Changing
- What is one of your secrets? Who knows about this secret? Who do you wish knew? From whom is it a secret? What might happen if this secret were known? What good might come of it?
- Think of somebody who only knows the public you. See yourself through this person's eyes. How would he or she describe you?
- Imagine yourself doing something you really, truly love. Now imagine that a private detective known for his brilliant powers of observation watches you. What does he write in his report?

- Explore a secret in your journal. When you're finished, read it once and tear it up.
- Write about a peak experience—a time when you felt truly alive and authentic.
- Take a walk somewhere in nature. Be on the lookout for an object or symbol from your walk that represents your authentic self. Write about it. Stay alert for serendipities or synchronicities involving your object/symbol. Keep track of them and write about what they might mean.

## Put Down Your Sword

Because authenticity shares a boundary with exposure, working with authenticity issues can leave you feeling naked and vulnerable; and because the unmasked self is not silent, many a notebook is slammed shut when vulnerability kicks into high gear.

Remember to pace yourself. If you find yourself reluctant to pick up your journal, you may be going too fast. Go back to a lower rung on the journal ladder. Feedback and support are very helpful. This work is powerful when it is done in a community of trusted others.

## Chapter Nine

# IDENTITY

A few years back, at Denver's Avenue Theater, an innovative stage comedy called *Greater Tuna* packed the house for an extended run. The cast was comprised of two men who played the parts of all the citizens of Tuna, Texas, including the dogs and cats. Some twenty-seven separate characters emerged, each with distinctive mannerisms, costumes, speech patterns, opinions, secrets, desires, foibles and wisdom. By the last curtain, the audience felt quite at home with the eccentric population of this place called Tuna.

Each of us has a Tuna in our psyche, complete with a unique, but not unusual, population of citizens. These inner characters have lived with us since we were barely able to internalize messages. They have been shaped and molded by heritage, culture, society, conditioning, privilege or its lack, religion, family dynamics and a hundred other factors. Like the pieces of a mosaic, these parts of ourselves contribute to the unique and complex picture of identity. They address the three fundamental questions we constantly seek to answer: Who am I? Why am I here? What do I want?

"Listen for a few minutes to the voices that run through your mind," says Sam Keen in *Your Mythic Journey: Finding Meaning in Your Life Through Writing and Storytelling.* "Listen and you will hear your father, mother, brothers, sisters, children, lovers, friends, enemies, teachers and heroes acting out their dramas on your stage."

Listen and you will hear your Inner Critic, Wounded Child, Macho Man or Wise Elder. You'll hear your Competent Adult, Loving Friend or Passionate Advocate. We all have bad guys and good guys, robots and geniuses, artists and slaves inside us.

These parts of yourself are called subpersonalities, or personas, or life roles. Like the actors in *Greater Tuna*, you dash backstage and change costumes when the changing situations and circumstances of your life call for it. Like any good actor, you may become so expert at playing the roles that it becomes second nature to live your life in costume.

These subpersonalities or roles aren't inherently bad or wrong. Some of them offer valuable protection; without them, life could seem difficult and dangerous. Just as you wouldn't walk across asphalt on a hot summer day without shoes, functional subpersonalities offer insulation from harsh realities. Outgrown or outmoded subpersonalities, however, can create more discomfort than protection. You might not walk across hot asphalt without shoes, but you also don't need lace-up, steel-tipped combat boots.

## Subpersonalities in Action

Reflections on first meeting of men's group: Walking into the waiting room I encounter two other men. I sit quietly in my discomfort, not knowing who these men are or how things will go. I look at my clothing and see how differently I am dressed. I sit quietly listening to the men exchange small talk, which seems to focus on what each does career-wise. I think to myself, "This is a struggle." A struggle for all men. Am I what I do? (Jeremy)

Jeremy's observation of his subpersonalities began in a men's therapy group. He was awkward and uncomfortable as the group began, and his awareness of the various parts of himself, which he named, was acutely in focus. As Kay Hagan notes in *Internal Affairs: A Journalkeeping Workbook for Self-Intimacy,* "Naming exerts . . . control. When you name something you recognize it from then on."

I enter the group room feeling anxious and unsure. I don my mask and bid hello. Ah, the "Distancer" has arrived, holding all at bay. As the focus shifts to me and I'm asked to introduce myself—the "Hurt and Vulnerable Child" struggles with the attention. I complete my introduction after much squirming in my chair as the "Child" and "Seeker of Truth" move back and forth. As the focus shifts and the pressure subsides the "Distancer" moves back into disconnection.

One of the cornerstone tenets of transactional analysis, a therapeutic style popular about twenty years ago, was the concept of psychological games that people play. Playing this kind of game is similar to operating out of a subpersonality: Both involve acting, thinking or behaving in predictable, often predetermined ways. According to transactional analysis, when you become aware of your own games, you begin to notice the games of others around you. In a similar fashion, Jeremy's awareness of his own myriad identities heightened his attunement to the masks of others.

Nearing the end of the group—the therapist suggests we set forth the areas we wish to work on. One member says he cannot come up with anything. I suggest authenticity. He claims to not understand. I ask if he wants an observation—he welcomes it. I say, "It seems like you're a phony." And dead silence falls like a wet blanket over the group.

Over the course of his therapy group, Jeremy's cast of characters became clearer to him. As he observed and named them, he added a thumbnail sketch of the most predominant beliefs, desires and motivations of each. The beginning of his list looked like this:

**Hurt and Vulnerable Child:** Frightened and unsure of his abilities, almost certain of being crushed one more time.

**Distracter:** Makes jokes to distract from fears and vulnerabilities. Gains attention through others' laughter.

**Seeker of Truth:** Desires honesty and connection with others, ongoing personal growth and increasing vitality and joy.

**Scholar:** Very serious and focused. Directed toward learning. Works hard to get information.

**Perfectionist:** Critical and relentless.

**Uncertain One:** Ambivalent. Wants attention but retreats from it.

**Dreamer:** Believes it's still possible to find love, satisfaction and peace of mind.

**The Powerful One:** Evolving over time. Tall and steadfast. Willing to lead. Takes risks. Provides reassurance and comfort. Reaches for the stars.

Some of the roles, Jeremy noticed, felt robotic or acculturated. It was as if he merely went through the motions, doing what he had always done or what was expected of him. At a deeper level, however, he began to develop insight about the protective functions of some of his parts.

I notice how I am inclined to do things on my own, not inviting the assistance of others unless absolutely necessary. This independence or avoidance of community is another area where the Distancer comes out. I'm not certain how much of this is just that male socialization stuff and how much is my own fear of appearing to need others to do life. I know much of my life has centered around remaining very independent—of not needing others. This most likely stems from constantly being disappointed by significant people in my growing years. I think I decided somewhere along the way that others could not or would not be there to help so I would do it myself. I struggle with asking for help or welcoming others' invitations. What an island I have become.

In a Character Sketch of a subpersonality he called the Nurturing Friend, Jeremy welcomed a part of his authentic self.

He really likes to talk and listen to his friends. He likes to surprise them with special gifts and cards and calls. He is often animated, excited, funny and full of things to tell. He loves to talk about his experience of life and to hear the experiences of others. He is supportive and nurturing and loves sharing a good meal with another. He thinks often of his friends, feeling the warmth bubbling up. He is loyal and available. He often goes the extra mile. (I like this part of myself. I think I'll keep it!)

Through the feedback of others, Jeremy checked out his internal experiences with the personas he projected. He found that discrepancies usually occurred at the level of feelings.

The facilitator asked group members for their first impressions of me. I got mostly feedback around being very direct and appearing confident. I said that

the confidence wasn't real. Inside I felt great fear and
insecurity.

Parts of his identity, however, felt completely congruent,
as if how he really felt and how he came across matched
up exactly. As he probed the roots of his Nurturing
Friend subpersonality, Jeremy recognized himself as a
child.

It must have been the Christmas I was five that I
got the Easy-Bake oven from Mom. It was
wonderful. Turquoise. I must have made every packet
of mix within the first several days. I had cakes and
pies and cookies. Mom just let me go at it with my
little oven, heated by that 60-watt light bulb. I don't
know whatever happened to that oven, but it was
definitely a hallmark of my childhood, the beginning
of that part of me that loves to nurture. My desire to
nurture, to bake, to feed myself and others was born in
a little plastic oven heated by a 60-watt bulb when I
was five years old. It survived the teasing and torment
of siblings and peers who said it was less than a manly
thing. Today I continue to bake quietly, without much
attention. And today I thrive in the joy I get from
making food and sharing meals with others.

As his authentic self began to merge with his public
identity, Jeremy found himself rethinking his personal
boundaries. How much of himself was he willing to risk
letting others see? Jeremy explored his topic of his secrets
first in the privacy of his journal, and then with the men
in his group.

When I think of secrets I think of the many I have held in the past, the few that remain, and the power they contain. I would like to think that I am very open, but that is dishonest. My secrets are locked deep inside an impenetrable box. Only a select few have keys and access. There's another box, even stronger and more secure, and I have the only keys. This box contains few secrets, but the power of them to evoke deep shame keeps them locked away.

Jeremy's search for identity continues. It is a bittersweet journey . . .

I hold back, still afraid to show you who I am. It's so different when I'm showing me and not my roles.

. . . but he is by now a seasoned traveler, and he has companions on the way.

Through this process of moving from the dark painful void of emptiness I have found light, yet also a richness of color. The colors of other men, the reflection of my colors in their mirrors and my own. This has allowed me to see more fully how my colors are not so different from those of other men. This has allowed me to not only show my rainbows, but also my thunder and rain. This has allowed me to know myself more deeply, share myself more openly, and run with joy in my new-found understanding. The door is open, no longer bolted with fear. It is open and I can walk in and out freely.

## Calling a Meeting of the Subpersonalities

Any time you are facing major life choices, you're bound to have conflicting opinions and reactions from different parts of yourself that seek to maintain homeostasis. When you're not tuned into the objections or reluctance of your subpersonalities, decision-making is difficult and you may even engage in behavior that seems self-sabotaging.

Try calling a meeting of your subpersonalities. You might think of this as an advisory council, committee meeting or, as William did, a board room.

William had just made the most important decision of his career. After a distinguished tenure as CEO of a manufacturing subsidiary, he resigned to pursue entrepreneurial endeavors. He had made this transition through executive coaching with a journal therapist.

In his journal, he first acknowledged and explored the many dimensions of his desire to move on. He identified the parts of himself that were involved in this decision and realized that their desired outcomes were sometimes in conflict. He planned his transition and rehearsed his departure. So far, so good.

Six weeks prior to his scheduled leavetaking, the parent company asked him to postpone his resignation date. William proposed a salary and bonus package for the extension. Just before the close of business one Friday, the company made a counteroffer.

Should he go for the sure thing and buy time to lay groundwork for his new venture, as his internal money manager urged? Or should he hold firm to his vision, as his entrepreneurial side advocated? William's ego was furious that his proposal was scaled down, but the voice of his doubt and worry was also loud.

At the suggestion of his journal coach, William called a Saturday "board meeting" with his subpersonalities. He started with a diagram of a round table where he sat with Ego, Money, Career and Doubt. Then he invited all of them to state their positions.

EGO: Ask for what you want. If it's not acceptable— screw it. After all you've done!

WM: But who did I really do it for? I did it for me!

MONEY: It does represent income that you're sure of, and the cash flow for the new business doesn't look that great for the first few months.

WM: I can't start worrying about money at this point. I can get a loan if I need to, and I'll earn more than what I need to get by.

CAREER: You have wanted to do this for a long time— you have everything in place. You have the support that you need. You even have clients ready to sign up. Go for it.

DOUBT: What's the worst thing that can happen? You might have to sell the properties and find something else to do.

WM: I'm good at what I do and compared to what it could be like, I'm miles ahead at this stage.

EGO: The staff needs you.

WM: It's time they fended for themselves. They are all capable and can do their jobs without me. It's not my problem any longer. It's time for me to let go and let live.

MONEY: You can make more than what you were offered even if you take a month off to regroup.

CAREER:  You can start setting up clients for the last quarter. This will be fun.

DOUBT:  Are you sure of yourself?

WM:  Yes, I am. I have everything I need to do this. I have six weeks to finalize all the plans, set goals and schedules. I'm ready. So how does the board vote? Stay or go? It's unanimous. I depart on schedule! Now, what's the next step? Set up a schedule for the next 40 days . . . write the letter and get it out of my head and down on paper.

His Monday morning journal included this entry:

The letter is done and faxed. What a relief. So now I'm really leaving as scheduled. Bon voyage! I'm always fascinated by this once I'm clear on my direction—getting it down on paper, in other words. When I "just do it" everything else comes into focus. I'm back on track, listening to tapes, updating my plan of action and feeling so relaxed it's wonderful. Got a call from Myron in Cleveland. He said, "You must be under a lot of stress." I laughed and told him I'm not under any stress at all. Once I faxed the letter I felt great. Close the door on one chapter and open a new one.

## PICK UP YOUR PEN

The Character Sketch and Dialogue techniques are naturals for coming to know your subpersonalities. Try this Structured Write to gather information. Start by closing your eyes and letting an image or feeling of this subpersonality come to the surface.

- Where in your body do you experience this subpersonality?
- What do you call this part of yourself?
- Make a thumbnail sketch of primary characteristics. These might include personality characteristics, temperament, physical descriptions and emotional qualities.
- What function or role does this part of you fulfill?
- How does this part of you like to express itself? (Examples: competition, dancing, yelling, sex, being the life of the party, sports, talking, writing.)
- What's your best guess about how and when this part of you was formed?
- What does this subpersonality want? From you? From others? From life?
- What does this subpersonality contribute to your overall protection and growth?
- What's this subpersonality's primary message to you? To others?
- What's your primary message to this subpersonality?
- Sketch or draw this subpersonality or a symbol that represents it.
- Try a journal dialogue with the subpersonality or its symbol.

## Questions

Who am I? Why am I here? What do I want? If you never did anything in your journal but answer these three

Springboards, you could fill up a lot of notebooks. Your identity would also start coming through loud and clear.

These questions are a lifetime's study. Don't tackle them all at once, and don't expect yourself to know the answers! You can expect greater clarity and increased awareness as you address these questions in your journal. You can also expect more questions!

Remember that flipping the question around into a Sentence Stem might offer more logical, cognitive responses. This isn't a hard-and-fast rule, but it's worth keeping in mind.

## Who am I?

Who am I today?
Who was I as a child? teenager? young adult?
Who am I becoming?
What is my identity?
What names am I known by? Who calls me by these names?
What parts of myself do I reveal to others?
What parts do I conceal?
Who have I been in the past?
What roles or masks have I discarded?
What do I value?
What brings me joy?
What do I stand for?
What are some qualities of my authentic self?
With whom do I share my authentic self?
What stands between me and my authentic self?

**Why am I here?**

> What is my purpose for being in this (emotional,
> physical, situational, spiritual) place right now?
> What do I have to learn?
> What do I have to teach?
> What experiences in my recent past have prepared
> me to be in this place?
> How did I get to this place? What events or circum
> stances led me here?
> Do I want to stay? For how long?
> Where do I want to go next?
> What does the present moment offer me?
> What do I bring to the present moment?
> What is my life goal?
> For what will I be remembered?

**What do I want?**

> What do I want for myself?
> What do I want for others?
> What do I want for the world?
> What do I want to do?
> What do I want to be?
> What do I want to have?
> What is the most important thing to do?
> What do I need to have?
> What do I need to know?
> What do I need to do?
> Do I have what I want?
> Do I want what I have?

## Chapter Ten

# WOUNDS

*I*t is a testament to the human spirit's relentless commitment to growth that some of us survive childhood at all. For all too many, childhood's promise of innocence, creativity, safety and wonder is yanked away and a legacy of conflict, alienation, misunderstanding or pain is left in its wake.

It's impossible not to get wounded. We're human. Part of being human is getting hurt. Life isn't fair. Because children are essentially without resources to provide for or defend themselves, life can seem especially unfair to and for kids.

No matter what the bumper sticker says, it *is* too late to have a happy childhood. You'll never be able to recreate your past and do it over. It isn't too late to have a happy adulthood, though, and one of the keys to freedom is coming to a place of closure with the past. This leads to empowerment, which leads in turn to new choices and freedom. As Gabriele Rico states in her book *Pain and Possibility: Writing Your Way Through Personal Crisis*:

> Empowerment does not lie in trying to escape these unpleasant states, but rather in learning to transform our suffering. Running away from suffering intensifies it; denying suffering intensifies it; wallowing in suffering intensifies it; blaming our suffering on others intensifies it. . . . What helps is to direct your pain into constructive acts, thus transforming it. Writing is one of those acts.

Through your journal, you can develop awareness, confront denial and tell the truth as you know it about your wounding, whatever it may be. Writing helps you gain useful distance and detachment from the painful events of your past. Without comparison, judgment or acrimony, you can simply observe and report your experience. In your own perception, you can even change your past. In *The Story of Your Life: Writing a Spiritual Autobiography*, Dan Wakefield puts it this way:

> The past can actually change. By remembering and writing down our past (and its meaning) and then reading it aloud to others engaged in the same process, we can sometimes see and understand it in a way that makes it different. Since our past experience only exists now in our own mind—it only "lives" in our re-creation of it—our changed experience of it becomes the reality, and in that sense we really do have the power to change our own past.

Unresolved emotional pain impacts the ability to react and respond to life in ways that bring satisfaction, pride, joy and peace of mind. Like old sports injuries, these pains may lie dormant until the next emotional front moves in. Then they flare up, restricting mobility and bringing unwelcome reminders of the timelessness of trauma.

When you use writing to heal the past, you give yourself a safe and private place to empty out. The simple suggestions in this chapter will offer a road map and help you get started. Should you find this work too painful or difficult to contain, seek out individual or group support before proceeding.

## Naming the Wound

Naming the wound is like lancing a boil. The toxicity is drained from it, and it can be cleansed and bandaged. The act of simply stating your own truth in your own words is inherently healing.

Sometimes it's helpful simply to inventory the hurts. An objective look back can highlight how beliefs and attitudes were formed, as well as how much healing has already taken place. This awareness alone goes a long way toward returning responsibility where it rightfully belongs. In this writing, Daniel reflects on his grandmother.

Vivid pictures and memories of a very unhappy woman. Who was she mad at, what was she mad about, what made her such an unhappy woman? To this day, nearly 20 years after her death, I don't know the answer. I am not sure anyone did.

As a child growing up she was very much a part of my life. She kept me while my mother worked from the day I was born until I was in the 11th grade. God, 16 years of my life with this unhappy person as my role model for women! At times I am still amazed that I've become the man I've become and that I've been able to slowly overcome many of the scars she left me with:

- Telling me I was a "bad boy" if I didn't tell her information
- Telling me that if I didn't tell her, it meant I didn't love her
- Calling me "Mama's boy" when I didn't do what she wanted
- Hitting me with a belt, a spoon, a stick and a razor strap
- Sending me to bed without a meal if I didn't disclose information to her about my mother
- Bribing a hug from me or getting me to tell her I loved her only when she would follow it with a reward
- Catching me masturbating and telling me "IT" would fall off if I kept it up. I never knew until I was in the seventh grade what an "IT" was and what it was that I was doing.

I never did know what she wanted in life to make her happy. I do know I didn't make her happy. For many years I felt responsible for her unhappiness until I was old enough to know it wasn't my fault. She was just an unhappy woman.

## Telling the Story

It is powerful simply to tell the story. To the extent you possibly can, release yourself from the expectation that you tell the story perfectly. Just write it. Let yourself go. If you don't know where to begin your story, start with the ending.

When Greg wrote this story in a spiral notebook, it was littered with scratch-outs and doodles. It was a powerful step toward healing his past.

I come from a long line of life-takers on my father's side and life-breakers on my mother's. That's how I ended up in the emergency room that night. A nervous phone call from my aunt announced that my father had shot himself in the head.

On this November night, having just been given an announcement of his second divorce, faced with the prospect of starting over again at 70, my father wrote a note, placed a gun to his temple and pulled the trigger.

Reluctantly, having had no contact with him for over 15 years, I drove to the hospital. The man who had denied me his love lay in an examining room, the life slowly leaking out of him. As I looked at him lying on the table through the glass in the swinging doors, an intern droned grim news in my ear. Brain dead. Motor functions continue. A litany of clinical details, cold, unimpassioned, hiding the fear and torment of a desperate act. My father lived another 24 hours. I found out later that he left a note. In a last effort at communication, my father poured his feelings out on paper. A lifetime of hurt, pain and regret. A final feeble attempt to find the voice of a life lived and forgotten.

When you are ready to explore the wound directly, be careful to select a technique that will help you contain the material so it doesn't become overwhelming. The AlphaPoem structure helped Paul manage a flashback to severe childhood abuse.

A little
Boy lost
Cowering in the
Dark. He is
Enveloped by the
Fear of the
Group that surrounds
Him.
I wish
John would come and
Kill all of them. They say they
Love
Me but I know it's
Not true, my
Only hope is to tell
People who are stronger, or not
Quite as scared as I am. I want to
Run to a
Safe place, but
There's no where to hide. Maybe
Under the bed?
Very soon the fear gives
Way to numbness,

Xhaustion sets in and I sleep, only to wake
Yelling for help, not knowing why I feel less than
Zero. I don't exist. Was I ever here? Am I real?

For Paul, the sense of "feeling less than zero" was abated through writing. A few months after he began utilizing his journal as an ongoing part of his self-management repertoire, Paul reported:

As I write about my life I'm starting to learn that my experiences do stand for something. I'm beginning to reconstruct the story of my life, which up until now has only been available to me in fragments of memory usually numbed out or dissociated away. Even though it's often painful to know the truth, it's also powerful to have mastery over it. If I know it and claim it as my own, then the truth becomes reality. And I can deal with reality a lot better than I can deal with not knowing.

## Seeing with Adult Eyes

Through the tunnel vision and limited focus of childhood, it is difficult to perceive parents or other authority figures as multifaceted beings. Instead, they are seen as omnipotent, godlike provider/punishers.

When you can see your parents with adult eyes, however, you can begin to appreciate the many levels of their lives. From the perspective of the peer, you can begin to create a relationship of equality and understanding.

A good way to begin is to imagine your parents at

the ages they were when your wounding was taking place. Often this mental age regression will result in looking at your parents at ages younger than you are now. This shift in perspective allows you to relate to the life struggles they may have been engaged in, given the economic, cultural and social values of their time. In this example, Michael gained insight into his mother's emotional distance.

> She's got her family now (two kids, not one), but it's a boy not a girl but that's okay too. She loves them and she loves him though there's something she's missing but she doesn't know what it is. She's the baby in her family where all the others are strong and independent and proud. If she can be that way too everything will be all right, she'll have fulfilled her role in her family. She was a lamb among the wolves. Her pride moved her into patterns of accomplishment and notions of right and wrong which matched theirs. She watches her son grow but she won't let him be who he is because she herself wasn't allowed to be who she was.

Greg turned to a family photo album to reconstruct a portrait of the young man his father once was.

> My father was a man who lived in a world he couldn't function in. [He was] one of twelve brothers and sisters; his alcoholic father left home and left his family to fend for themselves. Psychic wounds that would be played out later in his own family—me. An eighth-grade education. I don't know how he met my mother. I wonder who he would have been without her. A strong woman—too strong, in fact—she

guided his every move. Early pictures show him with his foot propped up on the running board of one of the year's hot cars. Somewhere I heard that my mother had "bought it for him."

He was young and smiling, wearing two-tone shoes and the look of a troubled, arrogant young man. How unsure of himself he must have been!

As he began to see his father as he would look at a peer, Greg noticed a softening in his own anger and frustration.

As I sit here looking at the rose garden, listening to the fountain, which serves as a background for the singing birds, I wonder if my father could ever have appreciated such beauty. Had the capacity to enjoy life been burned out of him at an early age because of the responsibilities of supporting his brothers and sisters? Education is a luxury when there's no food. Something I tend to forget in my comfortable middle-class life.

There was never any time to enjoy life. He had to support, work, fix. I desperately wanted him to love me. Sons seek redemption from their father's hands. I stand among the unredeemed.

## Creating a Relationship of Equals

Part of maturity is knowing that you can't change anyone else's position but your own. Another part is realizing that there are reasons people behave the way they do, and many of them originate in childhood. When you realize this about your own life, you can realize it about your parents' lives as well. We're all going about our lives as best we can, and usually we're making mistakes.

The dialogue relationship implies exchange, communication, commitment to listening as well as expressing. The Peer Dialogue (see pages 66–67 for a review) takes this one step further and also implies a commitment to understanding and resolving. From the perspective of a relationship of equals, healing can take place.

The Peer Dialogue levels the playing field by establishing parity between the dialogue partners. In imagery you can equalize the age relationship, power dynamics, characteristics that make communication difficult and everything else that would be helpful for entering into meaningful exchange. It's a helpful device to clarify positions on issues, provide behavioral rehearsals of actual conversation, and practice holding steady in the face of ongoing criticism. Michael's Peer Dialogue with his emotionally distant and critical mother began with familiar overtones.

ME: Why am I so fearful?

MOM: You don't have enough guts—you've done nothing with your life—I've given up on you. Most people in their twenties and thirties are busy with their families and careers—you, you'll just drift forever—after all, what can you say for yourself except that you wear skinny neckties?

ME: That hurts my feelings.

MOM: Okay, but it's true (looks hard into my eyes. Can I hold my own against her?).

Acknowledging his internal response of intimidation

and defeat allowed Michael to regain his emotional footing in the dialogue.

ME: We seem to be fighting each other. Is there some way we can have peace between us?

MOM: You make me out to be a monster in your head but I'm no longer the responsible one—now it's up to you.

ME: Well, that's somewhat true, but it's also true that you judge me instead of loving me, that you were in the power position in our relationship and that such judgment was a form of abuse. And that we've been in a family system where there is a lot of perfectionism and not much forgiveness. Forgiveness is what we now need, isn't it?

MOM: But if we forgive too much, then what are our values based on? Don't we then become flimsy and self-indulgent and purposeless? What is our purpose, after all? We should be strong, independent, and ought to accomplish something. What are you accomplishing? Nothing. If you have a problem, then you should get help.

Again Michael realized that the dialogue sounded familiar; his mother's responses seemed automatic and inflexible. The opportunity for resolution appeared to lie in his own empowerment.

ME: Well, I obviously won't get any help from you. So I'll go out into the world and get help wherever I can find it. I'll know when it's the right kind of help because I'm trusting myself. I'm grateful to you for bringing me into the world, and I hope to keep this dialogue open.

MOM: Yes, let's keep talking. I need some help too, and I believe you can help me.

ME: We're friends now.

MOM: Yes, we're friends.

By the end of the dialogue, Michael realized that communication with his mother might have a fighting chance if he were to approach it as the man he is now, thus balancing the power between him and his mother.

Death, abandonment or divorce do not end relationships. Relationships have their own life cycles. The Peer Dialogue with someone who has departed your life can provide invaluable assistance in helping the relationship move to another stage in its life cycle.

As he began this Peer Dialogue with his dead father, Greg quickly fell into an old pattern of defensiveness. The voice of his father gently reminded him to do it differently.

DAD: You seem kind of down this morning, son. What's the matter?

ME: Work mainly. Actually everything else is moving along—on its OWN schedule, of course, but moving. Besides, why should you care? You never did when you were alive.

DAD: That was always one of the problems between us, son. You drove me away as soon as I came close. What did you expect?

ME: A damned sight more than you delivered!

DAD: Look. This is supposed to be a dialogue, not another opportunity for you to take me apart.

ME: Sorry, force of habit, I guess.

DAD: It was/is possible for me to give you something of value, but you must let go of your bitterness toward me. As long as you

resist me, you will never be able to hear what
I have to say. I did/do have things to tell you,
but I can't stand the grief.

ME: Okay. I'll cool my jets. Let's talk.

After a discussion of the roles each family member had
assumed, Greg acknowledged that his belligerent behavior
as a child and adolescent was an attempt to gain his
father's love. In the dialogue, he was not only able to
provide for himself the fatherly advice and concern he
never had in life, but he was also able to receive feedback
about some of his own behaviors and patterns that no
longer serve him.

ME: I wanted attention from you desperately.
Early on I knew I'd never get it. I was willing
to do anything to get you to pay attention to
me.

DAD: Look. I came from a family with 12 brothers
and sisters, with an alcoholic father who
walked out on us and left us to take care of
ourselves. I had to quit school in the 8th
grade because I didn't have any shoes. I
worked hard my whole life in a job that
made me old before my time. I was married
to a domineering woman who conspired
against me with her children to make me
wrong. Don't you think you expected a little
much from me?

ME: I do now, but I didn't then. I knew you were
afraid of me on a number of different levels. I
beat you with your fears just like you beat me
with the belt.

DAD: You wanted more than I was ever capable of

delivering, and you were obsessively
relentless in trying to get what you wanted.

ME: Sometimes I still lose it.

DAD: Yes, but you knew enough to go get help.
That's what I'm here to tell you. You're smart.
Learn to forgive. Be gentler. Stop being so
rigid. Your rigidity is causing you to fall off
the wagon. If you don't learn to relax, you're
not going to be around to enjoy your life and
we'll be talking face to face instead of on
paper. I made some big mistakes. You can
spend your whole life hating me for them or
you can say, "He was a simple man." I
encourage you to get on with your life. Look
for positive things to be happy about. Work
with your problems head-on. Tackle them
and get them out of the way. Be happy. Stop
making up things to worry about. Life is
short. Live it.

ME: I know you're right. I know you did your
best. At times I feel all the hurt, pain and
frustration you felt. Life isn't simple. I am
unforgiving. Neither you nor Mom had the
insights I've had into life, nor the opportunity
to get better through recovery. It is time to
get on with my life. To grow up and realize
things aren't perfect. Thanks. I'll be checking
in with you from time to time.

DAD: Good. I'll be here.

## Moving On

Naming the wound, telling the story, seeing with adult
eyes and creating a relationship of equals will bring you a

long way toward coming to a place of resolution with your wounds from childhood. The last step is moving on.

In a journal group guided imagery to the House of Unfinished Business, participants were encouraged to meet up with a person from their past with whom they felt emotionally incomplete. Edward found his alcoholic, abusive father in the house, which didn't surprise him in the least; anger at his father had fueled him through years of therapy and volumes of journals.

The guided imagery continued with suggestions that he take this opportunity to say anything he needed to say to his father, knowing that his words would be received without argument or defense. Edward mentally drew a deep breath to confront his father about the years of abuse.

Instead, in his mind he wordlessly embraced his crippled father. When he found his voice, he thanked his father for three happy childhood memories—three incidents that had been buried under piles of pain.

A few months later, Edward drove cross-country to visit his parents. Upon his return, he wrote this entry that he calls "Litany."

My dad cried when I left home this time . . .
At one point during my visit, Mom said "I wish you'd spend some time with him; he looked so forward to your coming." I was reluctant . . .
he just watches T.V. now . . . I didn't know what to say to him.

My dad cried when I left home this time . . .
Did he cry because somewhere deep inside his damaged brain he is aware of how estranged we became? . . . Of how I hated him? . . . Of how much we missed together? . . . Of how he failed?

My dad cried when I left home this time . . .
I didn't know it at the time, but now that I do, I feel
guilty and am saddened . . . feelings I would not have
been capable of just a few months ago.

My dad cried when I left home this time . . .
And I cried too. I want other people to understand that
I am a product of my father. My history begins with
him . . . the beatings, the derision, the time he almost
killed me . . . all the events that surround him . . . they
are what make and shape me as I am today.

*But I never allowed him to be a product of his own
father* . . . I've never allowed him a history apart from
me . . . apart from our nuclear family. I never allowed
him a boyhood, a growing-up, a testing. I never allowed
him a sex life, a romantic life, a marriage, a failure or
success at things personal to him.

My dad cried when I left home this time . . .
He cried at the loss.
I cry at the loss.
Together we grieve the lost fatherhood.

## PICK UP YOUR PEN

- Begin by naming the wound. Make lists from these
  Sentence Stems:
  - The people who hurt me . . .
  - My wounds . . .
  - I was wounded when . . .
- Amplify the naming of the wounds by describing them
  objectively. Write without judgment, blame or censor-
  ship.
- Write Unsent Letters to your parents, siblings, teachers,
  authority figures. Remember: An Unsent Letter is delib-

erately a metaphoric one-way communication, so you get to say whatever you want to say without concern of how it would be received or responded to.

- You can also write an Unsent Letter to yourself at any earlier age in which you offer comfort, hope, reassurance and a preview of the future. Let your younger self know that things turned out okay and that he (your younger self) survived the experience.
- Write a Character Sketch of your parent or other authority figure as he/she was (or as you imagine he/she might have been) at your present age.
- Write a List of 100 Childhood Memories. Remember that it's okay to repeat. Reviewing the list upon completion and/or grouping the entries into themes will often lead to the next journal step.
- Draw the floor plan of your childhood home. Include as many details as you possibly can. Include the yard, garage, tree house, shed, neighborhood and other exterior locales if they were significant. Take a look at your map, and write about whatever captures your attention or imagination. This is a powerful device. Expect the unexpected.
- Write a Perspectives entry from the point of view of your parent/abuser/other significant adult.
- Write Captured Moments about your particularly vivid childhood memories.
- Family photo albums are powerful Springboards. Find a picture that moves you, and write about what it evokes in you.
- Write a Peer Dialogue with anyone who abused you physically or emotionally in which you can express the impact the abuse has had on your life, ask for accountability, and come to a place of resolution.
- When you're ready to move on, let your journal support you.

## Chapter Eleven

# VALUES

What do you value? What gives your life meaning and purpose?

These questions may seem easy. What are your answers? Family? Friends? Work? Money? Community? Recognition? Recovery? Creative gifts? Pleasure? Possessions? Learning? Take a moment now to jot down a few responses.

Now try these questions: How did you come to value these aspects of your life? When, where and from whom did you learn these values?

Woody Allen once said, "After twenty-five years of psychoanalysis, I have a brilliant understanding of my neurosis." Similarly, if you've spent much time in self-examination through therapy, recovery programs, support groups, personal growth workshops, self-help books, journal writing, and so on, chances are you've got a pretty good sense of the roots of your negative beliefs or self-sabotaging behaviors. At certain intensive stages of your process, you may have even felt as if you knew them so intimately that they slept under your pillow at night. But what about your positive beliefs? Have you afforded them as much attention?

At a backyard barbecue given by a friend who was graduating from her therapy group, I sat next to a woman I was meeting for the first time. As we balanced paper plates on our knees, she introduced herself by telling me that she was a fairly new member of the group.

"My therapist referred me to the group because about a year after I sobered up in AA, I started having flashbacks of childhood abuse, which explains why I started drinking when I was thirteen. They got so bad I could hardly work, but I needed to get a second job to pay for all the bills I ran up when my self-esteem was so low. My self-esteem was shot because I was so shame-based. . . ." Her story went on and on, filled with earnest details of her difficult life.

She paused to take an ant out of her macaroni salad. "Sounds like you've had some rough times," I said. "What do you do for fun?"

The woman looked at me blankly. "I don't have fun," she said.

Remember the anchor of balance? In addition to the stories of your sufferings, woundings and challenges, your journal will obligingly hold the stories of your celebrations, triumphs and blessings. An easy place to begin: your values.

## How Values Were Shaped

The Character Sketch technique is a natural for looking at how your values were shaped. One of the most notable features of the Character Sketch is its capacity to help you externalize and observe the qualities, characteristics and values that you may have internalized from the subject of your sketch.

Try a Character Sketch of a favorite relative or adult presence from early childhood. See if you can reconstruct a scene in your mind. If you find yourself adopting an unfamiliar writing style, don't question or judge it. In this sketch of his grandfather, Daniel's spontaneous use of present tense, gerunds and repeating words adds immediacy and voice to his writing.

> Sitting by the radio in his great soft chair he leans to listen, his great legs, bowed from riding horses, stretching out before him. Listening to the Lone Ranger, Dick Tracy and the Grand Old Opry. Cap resting askew on his bald head, his face weathered from years in the elements. His face rugged, but glowing with wisdom, love and stories. His great big crippled hands opening in a hug to me, motioning for me to find comfort and safety in his great big lap. As I climb up I feel his hand helping, his great arm wrapping around my body and his lips kissing the top of my head. As I settle in he asks, "Okay, Danny, what story do you want to hear today?" He always has a story or a game for me. That was my grandfather. God rest his soul.

What values did an impressionable young boy learn in the great big lap of his rugged, loving grandfather? When Daniel asked himself this question, the answers flew out of his pen.

> From him I learned that men cry, men love, men touch, men hug. I learned to work hard, to be honest, to respect your elders, to help my fellow man, when to be quiet, when to listen, when to stand up for what I feel is right. I learned compassion for animals and people. So many life lessons and great stories from a safe friend. Thanks, Grandpa. I love you very much, and you are still with me in spirit.

In late childhood or adolescence you may have found your first mentor or role model who influenced your career choice. As Jim reflected on the question of how he decided on education as a career, he remembered an important teacher.

> George Davis—my 8th grade homeroom teacher— strict, stern, fair with a real compassion for people and students. Mr. Davis (it still feels uncomfortable to call him "George") somehow taught me the love of teaching. It wasn't his guidance, any specific lesson, but just his presence that affected me so much that I knew I wanted to choose teaching as a profession. As I now reflect on him I remember that Mr. D. "influenced" me by letting me choose for myself, after setting a rich environment in which to look at possibilities.

One of your early jobs may have influenced your attitudes and values about the work ethic. Continuing his exploration, Jim reflected on the messages left by a role model who lived his dream.

> John Weber, bait dealer. He gave me my second job as a teenager—counting worms and catching crabs. However, what he left with me is the ability to be focused within myself. He was an entrepreneur in the late '50s who was quite satisfied with the role he carved out for himself. He was able to balance all his commitments to family and community, but also permitted himself the opportunity to follow his first love of fishing by opening a business known as JOHN'S LIVE BAIT. "Find what you want and then build the underpinnings to support it" would be Mr. Weber's message.

In *The Masculine Journey: Understanding the Six Stages of Manhood*, Robert Hicks identifies six stages of male development and emphasizes the need for role models or mentors at each stage.

> Wherever I am on the masculine journey, I need a mentor who is at least one stage ahead of me. I need this to provide a model of masculinity at the next stage and the encouragement I need to leave where I am and grow up a little. If I am a phallic college guy enjoying the sexual pleasures women bring me, I need an older man who may be a warrior in adult life, to show me how to channel or translate my sexual energy into something more constructive, like business or a career. When I am a warrior drawing blood from everyone around me, I need a wounded man to come

alongside and give me the perspective I need to see that one day I may be the one who is bleeding. When I think I am bleeding to death, I need a mature man to take some pity on me, bandage my wounds, and give me the hope I need to survive. When I am a [mature] man, I know what life is about, and it becomes so easy to isolate and just do what I want to do with my life. At that point I need a sage to give me a vision for my life. . . . I hope when I am a [sage] someone will be around to help me die well. Maybe that's when God alone is my mentor.

Not only do you need different types of mentors at different stages of life, but you may need to move into a different stage before you can fully appreciate and acknowledge mentors from earlier stages. From the perspective of Hicks's "mature man," Gary sees his "sage" father with fresh eyes.

My dad is 80 and won't be around much longer. This is what I want to say to him: You were my first male model. Much of what I learned—to be a male—was from you and I still carry it with me. Some positive, constructive, and some not so constructive. But Dad, the positives far outweighed the negatives. Your compassion, your sensitivity, your love of nature, your gentleness. The tears you shed for me when I was 17, walking alongside me as they wheeled me into the operating room—that unrestricted love. Thanks, Dad! Fortunately I am taking the time to tell him these things, in pieces, each time we get together.

## Updating Values

Sometimes your "values closets" need cleaning. You may have internalized certain values in your youth that were helpful for the prevailing circumstances but have since outlived their usefulness. Edward's celluloid heroes from childhood taught him the value of stoicism, an important survival skill for a badly abused boy.

> I used to love movies, particularly Westerns. When I was growing up I saw a lot of them at the theater on Saturday afternoons for 35 cents. I have often thought how much of my black-and-white morality was shaped by these films.

The Saturday matinees did more than excite and inspire Edward. They also provided safe haven from the rage of his alcoholic father. With his kid brother in tow, Edward escaped to the law-and-order worlds of Gary Cooper in *High Noon* and Alan Ladd in *Shane*.

> There was a haunted loneliness about both of them. So much that remained inside. They didn't beg the help of others; they didn't pour out their stories. They did their jobs like men. Gary Cooper was to face a gun-thirsty lot who were sure to kill him, even if he should have help, but there was little help available from anyone in town. Still, he would defend a town that didn't deserve his loyalty, or more, his life. It was a matter of law, responsibility, honor.
> Shane—there was so much unknown about him. When it came to defending ordinary, trusting, simple, loving people, Shane became the Christ-figure,

sacrificing himself, his dreams, everything for others. Even when he was wounded, Shane refused to be a burden. He rode off toward the Tetons, bleeding, but sitting tall in the saddle, with the call of a young boy the ultimate reward: "Shane, Shane, come back . . . I love you . . ."

Edward instantly recognized his own haunted loneliness, his own patterns of self-sacrifice, the discounting of his own bleeding wounds.

In real life I can want to be noble and sacrificial all day long, but what I really want is appreciation and acknowledgment. The loneliness doesn't work. Loneliness is really only lonely. And so I find myself trying to live up to the fiction, and in one way I succeed: "who I am" gets lost in the shuffle, it becomes a desperately important question to which even I don't know the answer.

In a cluster on "HERO" (see page 142), Edward uncovered more layers of his pattern.

The interesting thing about this cluster is that I have tried to live up to my image of hero, and I've done a pretty good job in achieving many of the characteristics that I listed. The trouble is that what I have chosen, the characteristics themselves, aren't really where I want to be now.

I really don't want the martyr role that has been taught so effectively by my mother. I don't want to be quiet and simply "take it." I want others to know some of the shit I experience, not just the good stuff. For some reason, I have equated "moody" with positive

feelings and respect, and I have done this act very well. Being moody is too lonely, however, and I formally renounce it.

Once he knew what values no longer served him and could "formally renounce" them, Edward could select an updated set of values.

If I had one line on my Cluster to claim and keep, if I could choose one of those lists to be mine, I would choose the line that deals with self-confidence and self-assurance, being at ease with myself no matter who I am or what others think. I want those values. They comprise my current definition of what it would take to be a "winner" in this life.

I often begin workshops by passing around a bowl of "angel cards"—tiny laminated cards with a single word written in calligraphy and a whimsical illustration. In a men's workshop, Justin selected the angel of STRENGTH. His immediate reaction was negative. "Strength! My father was strong, all right—strong enough to knock me around any time he wanted." I invited him to describe the illustration on the card. "The angel is hugging a tree?" he asked dubiously. Clearly any connection was lost on him.

"Just a suggestion," I said. "Hang out with STRENGTH today. As you write and share and listen, see if there are any positive aspects to STRENGTH."

In the next eight hours, Justin and his companions covered a lot of ground. They explored painful childhood wounds, checked in with the men they had become, wrote visions for the future. Every time a man shared his writing, the intimacy in the room deepened. The air in the room pulsed with raw power and vulnerability.

As the writing process closed I asked each man to summarize his learnings in an AlphaPoem. Justin wasn't the only one with tears in his eyes as he shared what he had learned about strength.

> Strength can be
> Tender? I
> Remember just the
> Evil side. I
> Never knew strength could be
> Gentle and caring. Until
> Today I did not know the
> Heart is also strong.

## Investing in Values

What if you could invest in values the way you invest in real estate or municipal bonds? What would you secure for yourself? These questions are the premise behind a fascinating and very revealing workshop experience, the Values Auction.

Everybody in the group is given $3,000 in play money and a list of twenty-two values (honesty, self-confidence, recognition, security, respect, prosperity, integrity and so on). Bidding starts at $100. Only the auctioneer knows the order that the values come on the block, so bidders are often caught off guard when they lose out on first choices, or when opportunities for bidding are passed by until a cherished value appears for sale. It's fast, frenetic, fun—and very revealing, as post-auction journal reflections demonstrate. Although Terry initially felt proud of the savvy purchase of "security," it soon became apparent that security alone was not the answer.

Hooray! Now that I have purchased "security" I can live a life without fear and worry. By buying security, I have purchased self-esteem. I can be secure with myself and with the world. I can *act* strong and courageous. I can *feel* safe and confident. I can *think* positively and I can *relate* well. I should be happy, right? Wrong! Sure, I may have security, but what about the things I don't have? What about *those* values? Maybe I'm being greedy, but I want it all. Perhaps at some point I could purchase the others.

Luckily, values aren't this easy to come by. If my values are really important, and worth believing in and striving for, then some effort must be made on my part to live my life according to these values. I value challenge, although I didn't buy it because I was outbid. Real challenge comes from living my life according to my values (even in the face of obstacles) rather than from me purchasing my values. This auction provided me with a life of security, but the challenges are gone. So *no*, I am *not* happy!

Steve's purchase of "acknowledgment" was quickly traced to a value rooted deeply in his childhood.

Why did I buy "acknowledgment" and what does it mean to me? First of all, because of my years as a child entertainer in show business, it means applause. That was the first kind of acknowledgment of my talents I ever received. It has been hard, ever since, for me to realize that silent appreciation is acknowledgment too.

As he examined the value he placed on acknowledgment, Steve realized that the child is father to the man—that even in his retirement years he sometimes acts from the fears and insecurities of the child he once was.

A lot of how I act, think and feel about acknowledgment has to do with feeling I've been unfairly, even deliberately, denied my fair share of it. When I'm overlooked or ignored, I still think (as I did when I was a child and couldn't get my parents to acknowledge my value as a person) that there's something horribly wrong with me. Then all the more I have to go into a performance of being accomplished, well centered, serene.

With clarity in place, Steve's next steps revealed themselves.

But all it takes to cure me of my "down" state is some subsequent acknowledgment of my value to someone, or of good work I've done, or of good service I've provided. My heart turns it all into the applause that the performer in me still loves. The next step is to acknowledge that most people do accept me most of the time, though they may not beat their hands together to show it. Maybe the final acknowledgment I'll achieve is to say to myself, "Trust yourself, you are a worthy person, and appreciated."

"The Waltzers," a tender moment Steve captured in poetry, reminds him of acknowledgment's gentle, gracious face.

I'm playing the piano
At Mayview Center, where old people sit out their
    days.
The white heads nod in time to my music,
A smile comes to creased faces,
And a few hands quiver or beat strong to the rhythm.
I play old waltzes, "Ramona" and "Alice Blue Gown,"
And they are swaying at some college dance
Or back in some evening at a restaurant long vanished.
And where am I in this luring, lilting,
Three-quarter time I create?
Back in a childhood where playing piano for people
    was beauty,
And applause, esteem, the spotlight's love I lived for.
The craft comes back to me—the smiles and
    beckoning looks,
As well as the chords and runs from a lifetime ago.
One quiet woman smiles and sways and caresses
The doll in her arms.
She and I waltz together in childhood's delight.

## Integrating Values

Some Native American teachings include the directive to live in a manner that will have an affirmative impact on seven generations. This includes honoring and respecting the elders and preserving their wisdom for their children's children's children. It was in this spirit of reverence for the teachings of the sages that the following journal entry was written. Like Al, we have never personally met Pete North. But through Al's loving tribute, Pete North's teachings can live for at least one more generation.

I have never personally met Pete North. But each year Pete, myself and hundreds of others share the same running experience. We all gather for the annual Butler 10K race on the last Saturday of June.

It is a day that begins early. Spectators armed with lounge chairs and coolers find their favorite spots. Runners of varied shapes, sizes and ability warm up, socialize and eventually conquer the challenging 10K event.

Me, I am somewhere in the middle of the pack. Pete North is somewhere at the end of the pack. He is the oldest runner to participate in and finish the race. Pete was 82 years old at this year's run.

While most of us are enjoying our post-race drinks, sharing our horror stories about "the hill"—Pete is still running.

The hunched running style is uniquely Pete North. And as the race nears its end, the same question is asked in our gathering: Can anyone see Pete North yet?

Finally the answer comes: There he is, turning the corner onto Main Street. He receives support from everyone he passes, as if he were their family member, their loved one, their personal friend. Pete progresses rhythmically towards his self-appointed goal, never breaking pace, but always offering a glance, a smile and a wave to his supporters.

One hour and so many minutes later, Pete North has completed the race. Many in our crowd begin to go our separate ways, leaving with a sense of well-being, accomplishment and community.

And without question, someone will always ask: I wonder if I'll be running when I'm that old? And without question, someone will always reply: I hope so!

Last Friday, Pete North was running along a rural highway when he was struck by a pick-up truck and fatally injured.

Pete North crossed his last "finish line" on Route 422 in Clearfield Township in Butler County at 10:20 A.M.

When I heard the news from my wife, I was saddened by his loss. Even though he was not a personal acquaintance of mine, he was a runner, a comrade, and a man worthy of my respect.

So the next time you begin to lace them up, think of Pete North. Offer a run and a prayer to him and to what he represented: Hope, inspiration, dedication and the joy of doing what you truly love!

## PICK UP YOUR PEN

- Sentence Stems:
  - Values are . . .
  - I value . . .
  - Without—(value), my life would be . . .
- Who shaped your values when you were a child? Who

were your kind teachers? What did you learn from them?

- Who were your mentors or role models as a youth or young adult? What do you remember them for?
- List all your heroes, mentors or role models by life stage: Birth to twelve, Adolescence, Twenties, Thirties, Forties, and so on. Leave two or three lines between names. Then write three descriptive words or phrases next to each name that express what this hero represented or meant to you. Do you notice any patterns?
- Which heroes have you outgrown? What values did they represent? How did these values serve you? Do these values continue to serve you? What replacement values have been or could be acquired?
- Cluster "hero" or "values."
- Dialogue with your heroes, individually or as a group.
- Which value or values would you buy at an auction? What would it mean to you to have these values as permanent acquisitions?
- Write an Unsent Letter to yourself from the value you most cherish.
- Who are your elders? What have they taught you?
- Close your eyes and imagine the heroes of your lifetime, or any combination of them, as players in a drama. Bring to mind the image of a life issue you are working on, including all the people, circumstances and events. Daydream about this life issue, imagining that your heroes are involved in some way. Let a little psychodrama unfold in your head, imagining the best possible outcome for you. Make sure there are plenty of obstacles. Write about your daydream.
- Imagine that each of your heroes gives you a gift. What is it? What does it mean?

- Imagine the hero himself as a symbol. What does he stand for? How does this symbol speak to your life as you are living it today?
- How are you a hero? Who emulates you? For what are you admired? How have you left your thumbprint on the world? What is your heroic journey?
- Imagine that you are the recipient of the Hero of the Year award. What individual, group or organization is bestowing this award upon you? Who is in the audience? What sort of a ceremony is it? Write your acceptance speech.
- How will you be remembered? Write your obituary.

## Chapter Twelve

# FATHERHOOD*

T here is a new trend in child-rearing, one in which men play a significantly greater role than their own fathers did. Sociologists and psychologists call it "participatory parenting" or "the New Fatherhood." In the politically correct and gender-bending 1990s, men are willingly and openheartedly creating relationships with their sons and daughters. They are determined to create a climate of healthy emotional bonding with their children that was, for the most part, lacking in their own relationships with their fathers.

---

*Two of the writers in this chapter have works in process based in part on their journals, and I am grateful for their willingness to have excerpts appear herein. Dr. Henry Roubicek is associate professor of communication at University of Houston-Downtown. His work in process addresses how journal writing enhances parent-child communications. Tom deMers leads men's groups and workshops in Boulder, Colorado. His work in process tells the story of his psychospiritual growth and his journeys with his daughter, Elena, through single fatherhood.

Some experts say it's hardly a modern trend; what we're calling the "new dad" is actually the "old dad" recycled. Notes Brad Sachs, psychologist and author of *Things Just Haven't Been the Same: Making the Transition from Marriage to Parenthood*:

> The absent father of recent generations is a cultural aberration. Up until the Industrial Revolution, men have traditionally been closely involved with the raising of children and have taken on many important tasks, such as vocational training and moral education.

But much is changing in this generation. In an Associated Press article, Mitchell Landsberg reports on a national survey of fathers. Although only one-third of the respondents thought their own fathers had changed diapers, 96 percent said they changed their own babies' diapers. Only half said their fathers had participated in parenting responsibilities such as taking children to the doctor; 86 percent said they themselves actively assume such responsibilities. And 75 percent reported they had taken time off work to care for sick children, although fewer than 25 percent said their fathers had done so.

When it comes to parenting, today's generation of fathers is venturing into realms for which they received neither training nor role-modeling. Complicating the picture for many men are the dynamics of divorce and long-distance fatherhood.

## The Heart of the Long-Distance Dad

I'm hovered over my kitchen sink in the house I can't afford. Too tired to cry and too scared not to.

Biting into a slice of cold, stale pizza I scan the room picking out Joshua's toys. He's gone. She took him away two days ago and I didn't do anything to stop it. I didn't want any more conflict. I didn't want any more pain. But at this moment, in my boxer shorts, in the darkness of my very empty house, I feel more lonely than I ever dreamed possible. And I know I'll feel this way for a long time. Maybe forever.

In 1989, two days after his ex-wife and toddler son moved a thousand miles cross-country, Hank picked up a pen and wrote. He wrote passionately, to his son, every day. Transcripts of phone calls and play-by-plays of visits. Pain, anger, struggle. He wrote it all. Facing battle with obscurity as a father, Hank fought with every tool at his disposal. One tool was a journal written for, to and about his son.

Hank teaches communication at a large southern university. But it wasn't until he began his journal that he realized the true value of communication—and how little he knew about it.

I need to find a way to express my own despair. The daily pain lodged deep in my heart will eventually debilitate my capacity to effectively communicate with Josh. I have to communicate to function. I can only learn this when I see my thoughts on paper.

Hank's near-daily writings capture small moments of shared joy.

You LOVE camp! Wow, do you love it! At first, you had some slight anxiety. By the middle of the first week you were saying, "Daddy, don't walk with me. I know where my class is . . ." I still went with you. But with your clear and dramatic gestures guiding the way, I made sure to walk *behind* you, while you confidently said good morning to all and gave "high fives" to the vast array of counselors.

He also carefully notes and frequently quotes verbatim his phone conversations with his son.

What a wonderful, precious talk this morning. The sensitivity you show is overwhelming, and today it was mesmerizing. You are studying words in school. I told you how, I, too, love to write down words and to learn new ones. You said, "I know, Daddy." You know me well, Joshi, which is what has enabled me to get through the past few troubled years . . . You are also learning about presidents. You knew that Bill Clinton is our president. You asked me about George Washington. "Did he die?" you asked. When I replied yes, you wanted to know, "Will he come back to life?" My heart sank because the topic of death has always been difficult for me. I tried to explain that death is a type of beginning. . . . You talked about your fish, Rachel, that died.

In addition to preserving the sweetly sentimental joys of fatherhood, Hank's journal silently welcomes the rest of the story.

Daddy is not well, sweetheart. I have a very deep depression that is debilitating me. My heart hurts and it stings because I can't come to see you tomorrow. It would not be good for you to see me this way. I couldn't even build up the nerve and energy to cancel my plane flight. I am crying now, very hard. I love you SO much and I miss you so much and I really can't deal with that very well. I feel much despair and hopelessness. I can't sleep and I feel helpless. I realize this makes little sense to you. I hope you never have to experience these feelings first-hand.

Whether he's bruised with pain or swelled with joy, writing offers Hank—and eventually, Josh—a glimpse inside a human heart.

The ticket stubs you see several pages back were from your first baseball game. What fun! You got a batting glove as a souvenir, ate lots of junk, saw lots of runs and had fun, fun, fun. The pleasure of being together is indescribable. The summer moved too quickly. I'm sorry I couldn't call tonight, Joshi. A flood kept me on the road five hours getting home. I love you.

Hank's fatherhood journals now span four years and seven volumes. As a legacy to himself and his son, he has captured a father's love, a child's growth, and a relationship reborn.

When you were "journal writing" along with me on Saturday night, you wanted to be certain that both the igloo and Jewish star were in this volume. They are, of course. When I showed them to you, you said, "Will they be there forever?" Smilingly I responded, "Forever and ever, Joshi." One of zillions

of sweet, precious moments that will be forever
embedded in my mind and engraved on my heart.

## The Struggles of Conscious Co-Parenting

There are many reasons why this new generation of dads
were themselves under-fathered. For some, it was no
more complex than the prevailing social mores and
values of the post–World War II American Dream: Dads
were breadwinners; moms were homemakers. Although
emotional bonding between fathers and children was
often lacking, the wound was at least a clean one.

> My dad never told me he loved me, but he never
> yelled that he didn't. He never hugged or kissed
> me, but he didn't hit me either. He didn't play ball
> with me but he came to my Little League games when
> he could. He wasn't around much when I was growing
> up, but he was an honorable man who worked hard to
> provide for his family. I can't begrudge the choices he
> made. He did what he thought he had to, and I
> learned the value of hard work and responsibility.
> (Harold)

Sometimes alcoholism, unemployment, marital
problems or other life stressors created a family
battleground in which children were used as ammunition
or targets. Instead of a failure to emotionally bond, these
children often forged a "traumatic bond"—an inexorable
connection between the abusive behavior and the
emotions of love and need.

It is well documented that familial abuse is learned

behavior. Perpetrators of domestic violence, incest and other crimes against children were almost invariably recipients of the same or similar abuse. Many in the generation of "new fathers" fight a dual battle: to overcome their own experiences, and to forge new kinds of relationships with their children. They must have the courage to break the cycle of abuse and refuse the legacy of violence, and they must listen to their hearts. They must rely on the unfamiliar turf of instinct and intuition to guide them in how to open their hearts to their children in ways that feel both foreign and vulnerable.

Conscious fatherhood requires men to take disconcerting leaps of faith into unfamiliar realms. For many fathers, particularly divorced fathers like Tom, the journal fills the role of empathic listener. In the absence of a marital co-parent, Tom finds that his journal provides a forum for processing, questioning, articulating and clarifying the many complex issues of parenting his three-year-old daughter.

Christine called to tell me Elena was protesting seeing me, didn't want to see me again. When Christine asked why, Elena said I was "silly." She often calls me a "silly daddy." She told Christine she didn't want to come to my house tonight. My take on this is that Elena dislikes separation from Christine and directs her anger at me, sees me as responsible for these separations from her mother. . . . Maybe resistance to me is related to the either/or connections. She gets Mom or Dad but not both. I know she hates that. If it doesn't end, if she continues a strong preference for Christine, perhaps I should give up some time with her.

Through its silent witness, the journal offers a resting place for everyday griefs and confusions.

Elena did not want me to pick her up yesterday. When I came in other kids at the pre-school said *there's Elena's dad* but she wouldn't look at or acknowledge me. I talked to her teacher for a while, then went over and picked her up. She didn't kick or tell me to go away as she did last year. In perfect silence she just grabbed my neck and held on. I rubbed her back and said hello, but I was very moved. Very soon after she said she wanted to be with her mom, and in the car, "I want my mommie" was accompanied by sniffing and sadness.

I repeated her words so she knew she was heard and told her that I understood and missed her mom, too.

At some point I said *I love you as much as a super big ice cream cone that fills the whole sky!* and she laughed, but soon fell back into her little resigned sadness. This is the sadness of children in divorce and it must be lived and felt. I felt it too. To feel things together is at least better than feeling them alone.

That night . . . that night she laughed that wonderful abandoned laugh of pure joy. And then she leaned over and whispered into my ear. She told me it was a secret. I said I couldn't hear her. She whispered again. I still didn't hear. *Say it to me louder,* I said.

She whispered just audibly, *I want you to come live with me and my mom.* That and nothing but that. No tears. *Maybe someday I will,* I said.

Fathers of daughters face a whole set of unfamiliar

and poignant issues. Profound and powerful instincts of femininity and womanhood emerge early.

> When she woke up Sunday morning, Elena told me she liked her mommy better than me. Just a sleepy, casually stated fact. *I like women better,* she said. *My mommy is a woman. I am a woman too. I don't like men so much.*
>
> I asked her why she liked women better, but she didn't have a reason. I asked her if she liked to be with her dad and she said yes. Then she added, *But not all of the time.*

A commitment to conscious parenting requires finding healthy and age-appropriate responses to emotions. The journal serves as container for feelings such as hurt, anger and disappointment. It also provides a place to examine beliefs, conditioned responses and culturally imposed roles.

> What children we both are. She doesn't want to be neglected and neither do I. I feel a tension when I care for her. I am not relaxed, and I realize it is because I fear she will reject me and say she wants only to be with her mother. Therefore, any lines I draw or discipline I impose can result in her opting for greener, less restrictive pastures.

As devoted as he is to Elena, Tom's life contains many other elements. His journal assists him in balancing these many factors and in clarifying the next steps he must take for his own psychological growth.

I am standing on the edge of a precipice in my life, a change that feels both enormous and necessary. It is paradoxical because I feel both that I must do it and that I can't do it. It feels like an alteration in the fundamental tenor of my life, like the death of everything I've clung to as personality. Yet it feels as logical and inevitable as death, a call to a different state of being that will cause me to look back at myself as a butterfly looks at its fractured cocoon.

## My Teacher, My Son

For the "new dads," one of the most satisfying aspects of fatherhood is the deep awareness and appreciation of their children as unique individuals. These fathers use parenting as an opportunity to learn and grow along with their children.

In the mid-nineteenth century, pioneer women routinely kept diaries and journals of the overland migration. In her introduction to *Women's Diaries of the Westward Journey*, Lillian Schlissel explains some of their motivations:

> The nineteenth-century diary is something like a family history, a souvenir meant to be shared like a Bible, handed down through generations . . . the history of a family's growth and course through time. Overland diaries were a special kind of diary, often meant to be published in county newspapers or sent to relatives intending to make the same journey the following season.

Similarly, "pioneer fathers" capture experiences, anecdotes and strength through documentation of their stories. Whether the histories are kept private, shared with family members, retained for future generations or shared with other dads, they offer unprecedented glimpses into the lessons of fatherhood.

Jim and Kelly have enjoyed a working marriage for nearly twenty years. Their well-seasoned partnership thrives on large doses of affection, support, humor and respect. Not only do they support each other's growth, but they also encourage the unique expression of each of their sons, Jamie and Michael. In many ways, Jim's journal is like a family album. He uses it to preserve special family memories, or to capture a particularly meaningful lesson or gift that he has received from his children. Sometimes he documents a significant awareness or insight. He uses his journal as a practice ground for working out conflict with the boys.

Jim's journal lets him observe and appreciate the many life lessons his sons offer. In one writing process, he was asked to bring to mind a "wise elder":

> Jamie, an elder at 16! My son's face kept jumping visually to mind as I was thinking of my elders. It seems almost paradoxical, but Jamie has highlighted for me the "work ethic" value. Through everyday example, he displays responsibility and willingness to not only carry through on commitments to others, but to continually search to improve himself in specific areas. Oh! To be so old, so young!

Sometimes the joy of parenthood must be given

voice. In this entry, titled "Michael's Gift," Jim memorializes a special time with his twelve-year-old:

 "Hey Dad! Could you do some cutting for me so I can save my fingers?" Michael's eyes sparkled with the anticipation of creating a special surprise for Kelly. A cherished gift began to take shape in our cluttered workshop. Pride oozed from my pores as I witnessed the endless energy exhibited in creating something unique for his mom. Long hours spent Friday night, Saturday and Sunday, designing, sanding, painting, researching and letting Mom know the boundaries of her travels. Is this the same Michael who has difficulty focusing on any household or school task for more than ten minutes?

Mike's face radiated confidence and the pleasure of giving to someone he loves. It was a priceless scenario that I was proud to share. Thanks, Mike!

Conscious parenting requires a willingness to recognize natural emotions, as well as a commitment to express them appropriately. In a dialogue with his tear ducts, Jim acknowledged his emotional nature and was rewarded with useful information.

J:   Tear ducts, I would like to spend some time with you to discuss some events of the last month.

TD:  Okay. Shoot away. Hope I can help!

J:   There have been a number of times in the last month where tears have welled up. For example, at Jamie's graduation and closure session.

TD:  Let's take the graduation. The Saturday

morning with everyone saying goodbye brought back memories of times with special groups. I guess the reflection and knowledge of what feelings Jamie might be experiencing did it. How did you feel about it? What was going on with you?

J: Partly, it was the sadness of closure. I guess it is difficult for me to let go of those treasured moments. However, part of it was Jamie's passage to yet another stage of his development and growth. Perhaps the dichotomy of exhilaration and fear. Excitement for the beauty and richness of the experience, but a touch of fear that our relationship will have changed. The father/son will always remain, but with a possible adult/adult communication. How will it play out? Will I recognize it? By the way, you surprised me when my eyes watered on viewing Jamie's memory album!

TD: Oh yeah! Part of it was being proud. The words his peers wrote indicated a warm, sensitive, fun-loving kid. Tears of joy.

J: You seem to be activated quickly lately!

TD: I've not given it much thought . . . but Kelly's father passed away five years ago this month. . . . Jamie's and Kelly's birthdays are coming up. I really don't know if it is any one event, a series of events or that I have a quick threshold for release of the "agua." Keep checking out patterns and feelings, and stay in touch.

J: It's a deal.

As a conflict management tool, Jim's journal offers an appropriate and well-boundaried space to blow off steam, discharge anger, practice communication and brainstorm options for negotiation. A letter shared with Michael opened the doors to meaningful communication.

Dear Michael: So much I want to get away from being the "heavy" in your life. I can't help playing the "dominant parent" role. I'm your father. Perhaps we could find a way for me to parent you so that you don't feel so hurt and angry and I don't feel so guilty. So, Mike, I need to talk, to really talk about working through some of these issues. I need to see your creative, devilish, sparkly side. I need to feel the lightening of the heavy negativity that I feel I bring to your life. Perhaps we could try a family journal or just you and I could try to work through our issues. Tonight's a beginning.

## Closing the Loop: A Generation Reborn

The past is healed in the present, and the journal preserves the present for the future. When a father/son relationship has been interrupted by death, the journal becomes a bridge between generations.

Al was only eleven when his father died. Eight years later, at the age of nineteen, writing a poem to his father helped ease his passage into adulthood, where his grief could be transformed.

Father, tonight tears of sorrow rained as I recalled your death.

Father, the wife you left has become a lady among

women. Your eldest son, still deeply hurt by your
departure. Your youngest son, too young to realize
you were even dead.

All your friends and their fine words. Still people smile
when I am introduced as your son. Guns saluted
you to your final slumber.

Father, now I salute you. No more tears of sorrow for
myself. Only tears of joy remembering your smile—
that smile I recall after too many years of forgetting.
That loving smile you gave me.

Father—it shall never leave me.

Another dozen years passed, during which Al graduated
from college, accepted a teaching position, fell in love and
married. On a special day, his father's loving smile
returned.

I dreamt of my father last night.
A soft knock called me to our door. I opened the
door—and there stood my father. Great joy filled my
heart as I hurried to greet him. As I did, a great light
surrounded his being—a warm smile covered his face.
Then he was gone.

I awoke that morning, July 9, 1988, to recall the
20th anniversary of his death—July 9, 1968.

For whatever reason, a tranquil, peaceful feeling
accompanied me that morning. I shared the dream with
my wife. We sat talking, relaxing in the sun—and she
felt the first flutter of life within her womb.

Al's son was born four months later, "A November
child/ Winter white, snowflake unique/ Nature's true
wonder," according to the journal, and Al now knows that
the greatest legacy he can give his son is the story of his
own life.

This may sound corny, but maybe journal writing is my attempt to leave some simple mark behind. It is my personal history, for better or worse. It is a personal history that probably won't be shared with many. But some day my journals will belong to my son.

## PICK UP YOUR PEN

- To warm up, write an AlphaPoem using the letters of the child's name.

    *JACOB AT TEN*

    Jumping and jiving like you've got
    Ants in your pants.
    Can't you stand still? Guess not!
    Oh well. You're a lively, loving,
    Beautiful boy!

- What family traits do your children personify? How are they like you? Their mother? Their grandparents? Other relatives?
- Family therapist John Bradshaw says if you have four children and treat them all the same, at least three are being raised dysfunctionally. How are your children different? From you? From each other? What are their unique qualities, talents, personality traits?
- Create a family legacy by telling stories of your children's grandparents, great-grandparents, other ancestors. Talk these into a tape recorder, or write the stories in a scrapbook.
- If you're keeping a "dad journal" like Hank's, frequent quick entries provide a running chronology and emphasize small details that otherwise get dropped out. Hank

writes daily, but he often spends as little as five minutes. Choose your "dad journal" with portability in mind. Five-Minute Sprint your way through grocery lines, traffic jams, reception rooms.

- Clustering captures details quickly. Illustrate with doodles or icons if you're graphically inclined.
- Make journaling a family activity. Offer notebooks to your children. Younger children can draw or color in theirs. Invite kids to tell stories that you write down. Ronald Klug, author of *How to Keep a Spiritual Journal*, bought his daughter a journal when she was eight.

> I explained to her why I keep one, and told her about the kinds of material she could put into it. To help her establish the habit of journaling, I have offered to pay her a nickel for every page she writes. (If she writes every day, it will cost me about eighteen dollars a year, a price I'm more than willing to pay!)

- Start a family journal—a shared notebook kept in a common area. Use it as a running dialogue of family activities, rules, events or discussions. A family journal is also an excellent message center for households with teens or young adults.
- Write Character Sketches of your children at each birthday or on a favorite family holiday each year. Illustrate them with photographs. Keep them in one family book, or keep separate books for each kid.
- Write notes to your kids. Slip them into lunch pails or under pillows.
- Use a family journal or community notebook for negotiation or problem-solving.
- Keep a journal scrapbook of Captured Moments. Illustrate it with photos or picture post cards. Conversely,

add mini-Moments to the back of photos in your family album.

- Make note of the life lessons your children teach you.
- What is your philosophy of parenting? What values do you most want to instill in your children? Where are you flexible? Where are your boundaries firm? As your children grow older, do you become more flexible or more firm?
- Breathe deeply into your heart space. Focusing on one child at a time, allow yourself to experience your emotions. Without defense, explanation or apology, allow yourself to write whatever comes. Continue until you feel complete. Remember to pace yourself.
- Explore in writing the times when parenting hurts, when your own childhood issues are triggered, when you rely on intuition because you simply have no idea what to do.

## Chapter Thirteen

# EMOTIONS

*T*he summer of my tenth year, driven by unconscious forces I didn't think to question, I created a backyard hideaway. It was tucked along one side of the house, secluded by lilac bushes, with soft dirt for digging and plenty of privacy. I retreated to my hideaway to examine and explore my confusing, often frightening, feelings. I grieved for the dog I didn't have, lamented my best friend's fickleness, wished fervently upon stars, trembled with anxiety, muttered rude retorts to my humiliators, crooned soft soothing songs to myself. Behind my foliage screen I faced and tamed my dragons. Then I dug deep holes in the earth and poured into them my grudges, hateful thoughts, bitterness, hurt, insecurities, anxieties and worries. Comforted by the release of my darkest secrets and fears, I carefully packed the dirt back in the holes and emerged from my landscaped cocoon.

By early adolescence a notebook had replaced the spot behind the lilac bushes as the container for my difficult and seemingly unacceptable feelings. Although I'm still partial to a good dig in the dirt, I'm now more likely to use my journal as a reliable place to sift through and store emotions. Judging by the journals of the men in this study, I've got a lot of company.

I keep using this word *thoughts* and almost forgetting the word *feelings*, probably because, as a man, it is easier for me to *think* than to *feel* or at least easier to express *thoughts* than *feelings*. Interesting because I can sure *feel* the variety of feelings arise inside me as I write. (Gary)

Feelings are complicated. Even thinking about feelings is complicated. How many feelings are there? One book on my shelves says four: glad, sad, mad, scared. Another says there are three hundred: 147 negative, 153 positive. No wonder we're confused!

Getting in touch with feelings can be a real journey of discovery, even if you're not quite sure where you're headed or what you'll find when you get there. Fortunately, you've got a devoted friend and confidant— your journal—to make the passage with you.

If you're committed to a thorough exploration of feelings, you may want to create a separate journal. A three-ring binder with divider tabs for different emotions works well; it allows you to punch and file information you pick up from other sources, such as workshop hand-outs, newspaper or magazine articles, pictures, comic strips. I like binders with inside pockets to catch miscellaneous papers. If your work with emotions is more eclectic, you'll probably be better served keeping your feelings entries with your other writing.

Some of the core emotions are anger, fear, grief, shame, joy, love and serenity. Stress isn't technically an emotion, but it's so universally experienced that we might as well call it one. Other feelings that weave in and out include passion, confusion, depression, trust, hope, self-esteem, guilt, courage and jealousy. There are, of course, many more.

When you name something, you can more easily have a relationship with it. If you do nothing more than acknowledge your feelings by name in your journal, entire new dimensions will open up within you for possible exploration.

For some time now I've worked with a client in individual journal therapy whose favorite emotions are "annoyed" and "irritated." Most life stressors are described in these two contexts. As we've probed what it means to be annoyed and irritated, we've found that many other feelings lurk behind those two descriptors. Outright anger, fear, anxiety, sadness, frustration, feeling out of control—all of these are lumped under annoyance and irritation. This awareness allows my client to tentatively try on new names: "I'm irritable today, but maybe I'm also afraid." Ah!

## Tracking Feelings in the Journal

Just because you don't mention feelings by name doesn't mean they aren't present. Sometimes you have to read between the lines. Try going back through your journal entries and "deducing" the emotional content. Write feeling words in the margins. If you're not sure, take your best guess.

Remember the men who filed by my office mirror? Let's practice reading between the lines of their observations (see pages 94–95). To demonstrate this I'll borrow a device from dreamworker and author Jeremy Taylor, who advocates that any observation about another's dream be prefaced with this statement: "If this were my dream . . ."

> I'm getting older, but I still look good. I like my looks. I've matured. Maybe I also like how I am inside.

If this were my journal entry, I'd feel some pride at being a good-looking guy. I'd also have a sense of pride—and maybe some relief or gratitude as well—about liking who I am. But if this were my journal entry, the pride and self-esteem would be tempered with just a hint of sadness at getting older. I'd be a little scared of what the future might bring.

> Gray hair, thinning, "giant economy size" forehead. At least I didn't break the mirror! Good thing I couldn't see my paunch!

If this were my journal entry, I'd look underneath the self-deprecating humor and find some anxiety and vulnerability. I'd be aware of how uncomfortable it feels to try and look inside. Maybe I'd even want to turn and run.

> This was harder than it sounded. I can barely look myself in the eye. What do I think I'll see?

Reminds me of that poem about facing the man in the mirror each day. Spooky.

If this were my journal entry, I'd feel vulnerable and unsure. Worried that I might be opening myself up for more than I'd bargained for. I might also feel a small thrill of excitement at the anticipation of the "white water" ahead.

Although much of the feeling in a journal entry is hidden, there are times when you'll name feeling words right out loud. Try underlining or highlighting the words that describe emotions. William's Monday-morning journal entry after his "board meeting" with his subpersonalities (see pages 112–113) contains quite a few feeling words or phrases.

What a relief. . . . I'm fascinated . . . feeling so relaxed. . . . I laughed and told him I'm not under any stress. . . . I felt great.

Try keeping a running list of feeling words or phrases in the back of your notebook. Include both the emotions you've named directly in your writing and the ones you've intuited by reading between the lines. You just might be surprised at how many feelings you can find and name!

## The Feelings Worksheet

Feelings are natural and organic. They live in your body. You probably know more about them than you might think. A good first step is to collect the information you do have. If this feeling had a color, what would it be? How about a shape? Texture? Temperature? Size? If this feeling were a weather condition, what would it be? Where in your body does the feeling hang out? If it could talk, what would it say? What would you say back to it? When are three instances when you distinctly remember having this feeling? What do you usually do when you have this feeling? How do you deal with it? How could you use this feeling more productively? How do you block yourself from knowing more about the feeling? If you truly let yourself feel the feeling, what might happen? What are three things you're willing to do, starting now, to change your relationship to this feeling? Whom can you ask for support?

These questions can be found on a blank Feelings Worksheet on pages 178–179. Enlarge this on a photocopy machine, or enter it into your own computer.

The following journal ideas will help you access and explore your feelings.

## PICK UP YOUR PEN

- Make a list of the feelings you know well, recognize instantly and hang out with regularly. Make another list of all the feelings you are acquainted with but only somewhat. Make a third list of feelings that you don't relate to or understand.
- Each night before you to go bed, decide on a feeling you'd like to experience the next day. Write this feeling in your journal as the "emotion du jour." As you go to sleep, think about the feeling you've chosen. How would you recognize it? What would you be doing?

How would your physical body reflect this feeling (laughing, open body posture, quiet, making eye contact and so on)? Who could "reality check" you about this feeling? Each night, write a Five-Minute Sprint using the Springboard, How did I experience (feeling) today?

- Write a Character Sketch of a feeling. Describe it as a person, animal or other living object. Visualize its dress, age, physical presence, emotional wants and needs, message to the world, how it got that way, when you first became acquainted, and so on.
- Cluster the feeling to better understand your personal history and associations to it.
- Write an AlphaPoem about the feeling, using either the entire alphabet or the letters of the feeling. Here's an AlphaPoem on grief from the journal of Taylor, an art therapist who counsels men diagnosed with HIV and AIDS.

A crushing
Bellow
Calls from deep inside
Driving to be heard
Ever so
Frightening, ever so demanding,
Grief
Hits with a tornado's force,
Igniting the fire,
Jarring the senses,
Kicking the safety and comfort away.
Lamenting the loss, the pain
Mere words cannot begin to describe,
No, words cannot do justice to the
Once-held, once-loved, always-remembered
Person, people, passion. 'Tis
Queer this experience

Required in life.
Solace can be found
Tonight, tomorrow—
Until once again the
Vine of death crawls in my
Window, playing the
Xylophone of harmony lost.
Yes, I will go on. You will never be
Zero.

- Talk to the emotion through Dialogue. You'll likely be surprised at how much you'll have to say to each other. Ask the feeling what it's trying to express, how it serves you, what it wants from you.
- When you notice yourself having a strong emotional response, write a Captured Moment. Surround the emotional moment with the corresponding sensory details.
- This is a good process to do in a group, but you can also do it by yourself. Go through old magazines until you find a picture that evokes an emotional response. Mount it in your journal and write about what it stirs in you.
- While you've got the magazines out, try a collage about a particular feeling, or about emotions in general. Collage is an excellent way to bridge into verbal expression. Since other people often see connections and themes that you might miss, do this in a group, or invite a trusted friend to process with you.
- Emotions respond well to poetry. Start with an image that describes or defines your emotional state.
- Draw your emotion. Represent it in color, line or shape. If you aren't proficient at artistic renderings, try working in artist's chalk. Smudge the colors with a tissue or your fingers.

## FEELINGS WORKSHEET

The feeling I wish to work with is _____

If this feeling had a color, it would be _____
_____

If this feeling had a shape, it would be _____
_____

If this feeling had a texture, it would be _____
_____

If this feeling had a temperature, it would be _____
_____

If this feeling had a size, it would be _____
_____

If this feeling were a weather condition, it would be _____
_____

The place in my body where this feeling hangs out is _____
_____

If this feeling could talk, it would say _____
_____

And it would also say _____
_____

What I want to say back to this feeling is _____
_____

Three instances when I distinctly remember having this feeling are
1) _____
2) _____
3) _____
Usually when I have this feeling I _____

Or else I _____

The way I deal with this feeling is _____

_____

And I also _____

_____

The way I could use this feeling productively is _____

_____

And I could also _____

I block myself from knowing more about this feeling because _____

_____

I'm afraid that if I let myself truly feel this feeling, I would _____

_____

And that would mean _____

_____

But what I really want is _____

_____

And _____

_____

Three things I'm willing to do, **starting now**, to change my relation-

ship to this feeling are _____

1) _____

2) _____

3) _____

I will ask for support from _____

## ANGER

*A Word About Destructive Anger*

In his book *Men's Work: How to Stop the Violence That Tears Our Lives Apart,* community activist Paul Kivel outlines the two tasks men face in converting destructive anger to healthy anger:

> As men we have two crucial tasks before us in order to use anger powerfully and not abusively. The first is to separate anger from the many other feelings we were never allowed to express. We need to acknowledge, feel and express the love, caring, sadness, hurt, dismay, affection, gentleness and hope we carry with us. As we separate these feelings from the anger, the second task becomes understanding where our anger comes from, what we can do about it, and how we can express it in positive ways.

The journal is an excellent tool for facilitating the two tasks Kivel describes. It is important to note here that by itself, the journal may not be an adequate tool for someone who is prone to destructive anger and violence. People who have difficulty managing their impulses may act out anger through emotional, physical or sexual abuse of others. Writing about the angry feelings might help work them through, but it also might make the feelings seem even more justified and actionable. Almost every community has programs available for men who are exploring new and healthier directions for their destructive anger. The journal can be a vital and helpful adjunct to treatment sought from a therapist, men's group, recovery program or social service agency.

## How Anger Looks and Feels

> Sometimes I hear people say they don't remember what it was like before AIDS. I say I don't ever want to forget. This holocaust only drives me harder and faster. . . . I don't know if I want to bear witness to the destruction of lives any longer. I don't know if I can hear of one more diagnosis of HIV. I don't know if I can go and get tested one more time and walk through the anxiety and fear of maybe it's my turn now. I want it to stop! I want to wake up and find it has only been a terrible nightmare! I want my friends back! I want to love again! (Taylor)

Anger is a response to feeling violated or intruded upon. Its milder forms (irritation, annoyance, frustration) may come as a result of your perception that someone else has shown a lack of regard for your feelings, lifestyle, property or beliefs. Its more extreme and potentially destructive forms (rage, outrage, violence) usually come about as a result of a perceived or real threat that something you value will be taken away, damaged or compromised. Healthy anger is usually an indication that your boundaries have been violated in some way.

Anger creates a high state of tension in the body. Physically, you may feel tense, with tight muscles and a body posture that is poised for action. Anger often feels hot and consuming. There is usually a strong impulse to discharge physical energy aggressively and intentionally, such as striking out with the arms (hitting, stabbing, throwing) or with the legs (kicking, running) or verbally (yelling, tongue-lashing). Sometimes the impulses are turned inward and self-destructive thoughts or feelings come up strongly.

Anger is often accompanied by mild to intense irrationality and single-mindedness. You may lose your ability to see the bigger picture. There is also sometimes an accompanying sense of paranoia, suspicion or persecution.

Frequently anger overlays intense feelings of fright or anxiety.

## The Primary Tasks for Anger

The first step, of course, is to recognize and acknowledge that you're angry. The next step is to ventilate the feeling in safe, appropriate and nonviolent ways. Communicating your anger is excellent, but sometimes it's easier to communicate without aggression or attack when you've discharged the first layer of energy. Exercise or movement offers release. Self-management techniques such as deep breathing, taking a voluntary time out, using visualization, and writing through your anger offer useful distance and perspective. Finally, a primary task is to learn how to use anger as a barometer and positive messenger.

## Journal Work with Anger

If there is intense energy to be discharged, journal writing will likely not provide enough physical release. If you have a strong desire to rip or stab the paper, try any sort of safe and available physical activity—running, pacing, stair-climbing, a fast walk or any sports activity until the first layer of energy is released.

Ripping (old!) phone books is a good upper-body release that makes a satisfying mess. To add lower-body release, crumple old newspapers and stomp on them.

Once you have discharged enough energy to focus on writing, let yourself release control of how you physically write. Your penmanship might shift to a larger, more sprawling style or a much tighter, more compressed style. The pressure of your pen might be much harder. You might print instead of writing in cursive. You might use page boundaries in different ways. For instance, you might write without margins or with wider-than-normal margins. You might not stay on the lines, or you might write in chunks or angles across the page.

At the beginning of your entry, try writing three feeling words that describe your internal state. Write three more feeling words when you're finished. This lets you track how your feelings shift with time and process.

Often you can write through an episode of anger by utilizing Free Writing and giving yourself permission to write anything at all. Frequently these entries will sound illogical or irrational; they may bounce around among subjects, ideas, thoughts and feelings. That's okay. Postpone rereading until you've calmed down. If Free Writing intensifies your anger, drop back to a lower rung on the journal ladder.

## PICK UP YOUR PEN

- Lists of 100 (100 Things I'm Angry About; 100 Things I Want to Say or Do; 100 Things I Could Do With This

Feeling) invite short, nonlinear, repeated responses—all useful when you're feeling one-dimensional.

• Write a series of Unsent Letters to whomever/whatever you're angry at. Once is generally *not* enough! Literally write the same letter over and over until you find yourself calmed, exhausted or bored.

• Keep an Anger Log to identify the patterns of your anger. Include columns such as: how I felt; what happened just before; what I did next; what I did/didn't do to deal with feelings; outcome.

• When you are not angry, write a list of coping or stress management strategies. Tape it to the refrigerator or the bathroom mirror so it will be available when you need it. Use it!

• Especially if anger is problematic for you, write ongoing Dialogues with Anger.

• Make journal notations of your progress in recognizing and managing anger. Highlight or index these notes so you can review your progress.

## FEAR

While taking a break from yard work, I called M to check in on him. He hasn't been feeling well. He didn't sound very good. He started talking about tests and I went numb. I knew what he was going to say. M told me his HIV test came back positive. My numbness grew as I pictured the walls moving inward. One more of my close friends is diagnosed, this dreadful and terrifying disease is getting closer and closer. (Taylor)

## How Fear Looks and Feels

Fear is a response to a threat of harm or to the presentation of a risk or challenge. It's a normal reaction to any situation in which there is an expectation, real or imagined, that something bad is going to happen. It's also a normal reaction to feeling inadequately prepared for a task or challenge. Fear is a frequent response to change. The fear continuum ranges from nervousness, worry and apprehension to terror and panic. Vulnerability is a special subset of fear that is characterized by an often uncomfortable sense of exposure and openness.

Depending on your unique physiological fight-or-flight response, fear may drain your energy and leave you feeling vacant and immobilized, or it may charge you up into a state of nervous, restless agitation. You may find yourself drawing your body into huddled, protective postures. Your breathing may become shallow.

Again depending on your individual response, fear may push you into aggressive confrontation, or you may feel victimized and want to run away or hide. If you have a history of psychological trauma (such as childhood abuse, combat duty, catastrophic accident or natural disaster), it's likely that triggers to the trauma will render you dissociated from other feelings and the ability to think clearly. At the same time you may be completely absorbed in the timelessness of the perceived present moment. This is the phenomenon known as flashbacks.

## The Primary Tasks for Fear

Some of the tasks of fear include learning the difference between crippling anxiety and healthy, rational fear; how to acknowledge vulnerability; and how to discern positive, purposeful, life-enhancing risks from dangerous, trauma-reenacting "setups". Additionally, it's important to know how to tune into your unique individual sensory/bodily fear responses and interpret their messages.

## Journal Work with Fear

Use your journal to rationally challenge the sources of your anxiety through worst-case/best-case scenarios. When you become immobilized with fear, ask yourself: What's the worst thing that can realistically happen? Can I risk that? And if I risk that, what's the worst thing that can realistically happen? Keep going until you reach the bottom line. Do the same for the best thing that can realistically happen. Decide in advance what you mean by "realistic."

If you are chronically worried or anxious, try creating a two-week worry window. Anytime you are gripped with worry or doubt, narrow your focus to an action step you can accomplish in the next two weeks. Keep a list of these worries and action steps so you can document your movement through fear.

When you're anxious or fearful, you're likely to pull in the right margin of your writing. Concentrate on pushing the margin out near the end of the page. Imagine yourself pushing through your fear as you do this.

When fear calls us to risk-taking action, it can be a powerful, positive motivator. To transform fear into power, ask yourself this journal question: *What can I find in this situation that excites or inspires me?* Fear fueled with positive excitement gets results.

Many techniques from rational-emotive and cognitive therapies, such as challenging irrational ideas and thought-stopping, can be especially helpful for fear, worry and anxiety. See the Resources section for more information on these techniques.

## PICK UP YOUR PEN

- Sentence Stems:
  - Fear (or anxiety, worry, dread, panic, and so on is . . .
  - I often experience fear when I . . .
  - Fear stops me from . . .
- Write a Character Sketch of your fear, having first personified it through imagery.
- Write a List of 100 Fears. Look for themes. How many of the fears on your list could be classified as worries? How many are irrational? How many seem to have some basis in reality? Which ones can you actually do something about?
- Dialogue with Fear, Vulnerability or other allied emotions.

## GRIEF

It's been weeks since I've written. My thoughts have often moved toward my journal though my energy has led me to rest and other diversions. My friend S has now lost his ability to walk and his speech has become labored and faint. He has reached the final stages of AIDS. His spirit continues to fade with his many physical debilitations, glimpses of my former friend appear ever infrequently. I catch words that reveal his struggle and his desire to make it easier for those concerned. His "okay" sounds so contrived as if to say—"I don't know how long I can continue this fight." I struggle with my desire to visit and say goodbye, coupled with my fear of not recognizing my friend. I don't know if I can look into those sunken, tired and pain-filled eyes. To look at his shrunken, frail and failing body that a short time ago was close in appearance to my own. I don't know if I can bear the emptiness, the loss of hope, the fading lightness, and the loss of joy and life. I suppose at some level I prefer to retain the image of the past, of a vital, loving and creative man who brought laughter, dreams and friendship to my life. I want to remember his fantasies, desires and hopes. I want to remember the good times we shared. I'm not ready to lose another friend. I'm not!

I am so numb from the many losses that continue to mount with each passing year. I feel frozen in sadness, my tears unable to run their usual course. Are they dry from falling so frequently, or are they failing to fall from sheer disbelief? I no longer know. (Taylor)

## How Grief Looks and Feels

Grief is a natural response to the loss of something meaningful. This can be a person or relationship, a lifestyle, a dream or vision, a job, health, innocence or anything else that is emotionally valued.

People in grief often appear dazed or distracted. Your facial expression may be frozen and masklike. Breathing is often shallow and constricted. The preoccupation with internal focus may result in mild to severe physical clumsiness.

Inside, grief feels awful. No wonder people try so hard to avoid it! The heart area feels raw, heavy and tight. Short-term memory may be impaired. It's hard to focus. You may try to distract yourself from your preoccupation with the loss through any number of behaviors. There is often a sense of gloominess, pessimism or internal darkness. You may feel easily overwhelmed, exhausted and depressed. The world may seem unsafe; you may feel abandoned by God. You might feel as if your life has irrevocably changed for the worse, and nothing will ever be the same again. Doubt, indecision and insecurity may eat away at your self-confidence and self-esteem.

In the shock and denial stages of grief, you are likely to have an unreal sense of normalcy during which you surprise yourself by how calm you are or how well you function. You may decide, for instance, that there's no reason to take time off from work or otherwise adjust your routine. You may even feel guilty because you don't seem to be affected by the loss. These are normal feelings for this stage.

## The Primary Tasks for Grief

The first and foremost task is to allow the feelings to surface. They will not go away by themselves, and there is never a convenient time for them. It's helpful to remember that feelings are transitory. You won't feel like this forever.

Other tasks are to follow along while grief moves through its various stages (shock/denial, anger, bargaining, depression, acceptance) and to allow for expression at each stage. You don't have to worry about "doing" these stages; the stages will "do" you.

Another task of grief is to remember the departed. Let yourself be supported by your friends and family. If you can ask for support when you need it, great. If not, accept offers.

## Journal Work with Grief

When grief is new, feelings are so close to the surface and pain is so raw that short, structured techniques from the lower rungs of the journal ladder are most helpful. Time feels like an enemy when you're adjusting to a loss, so it's comforting and reassuring to document your movement through it. You can do this easily by numbering the pages of your journal and only writing on one side of the page. Also try writing on every other line. This isn't to use up your notebook faster; it's because the grip on your pen is likely to be less firm, and your handwriting might be larger, loopier or more sprawling than usual.

Because your memory may be affected, keep to-do lists, and keep them right in your journal or day planner. Loose papers are easily misplaced. Writing gives a sense of task-orientation and accomplishment when immobilization sets in, so give yourself lots of writing projects. But keep them brief—a list of ten things, a plan for the next few hours.

## PICK UP YOUR PEN

The first few suggestions are for anticipatory grief. This is when you grieve an imminent loss, such as when someone you love has a terminal illness.

- Unsent (or sent) Letters are good for communicating things you might have difficulty saying out loud.
- A community journal cocreated with caregivers and loved ones is a precious gift for those left behind.
- Invite your loved one to record orally a life review or mini-autobiography. Check the library for books on autobiographical writing for ideas on format and approach.
- Write Lists of 100: What I Love About You; What I Want to Thank You For; Times I'll Remember.

These suggestions are for active grief, when you're working through the stages of grief toward resolution and acceptance. It does not have to be a person you are mourning; you can also mourn the loss of health, dreams, lifestyle, pet, job, and so on.

- Write three words describing your feelings at the beginning and the end of every entry. This helps you track your feelings over time.
- Write Unsent Letters to and from, and Dialogues with, the sources of your mourning.
- Write Captured Moments to explore your mental snapshots about the loved one, the process of dying, or any other loss you're grieving.
- Brief daily entries help note movement through time. Try a one-year diary. Small progress adds up.

The next two ideas are for stored-up grief that has accumulated over time. The suggestions for active grief also apply.

• Latino cultures practice *descansos*, a custom of marking the place of loss with a cross. You can practice *descansos* by making a loss life-line. On a big sheet of paper, draw a horizontal line. Make a mark for every year of your life. Above and below the line, fill in specific losses at specific ages. Mark each loss with a cross. For big losses, make big crosses. For small losses, make small crosses. Have colored markers, pencils or crayons handy and decorate your crosses.

• Write a list of 100 Things I Have Never Grieved, Mourned or Acknowledged the Loss Of.

## Thoughts on Feelings*

I attended a men's meeting last night. It was snowing hard outside as we passed a talking staff. D. picked it up and didn't speak for a time. Then he reviled a woman across the street from where he lives. She cut down a maple tree in her front yard, over a hundred feet tall, he said. You couldn't get your arms around it, there before the houses on the block were built, his view out the front window, a being of grace and beauty for everyone who lived there, destroyed. He guessed they probably built the block around that tree.

His anger, his tears, were beautiful. Moved us all deeply, the heart of the evening. Everything is to be learned from a man who feels.

What I understand is in avoiding grandiosity, in

---

*By Tom deMers of Boulder, Colorado. From a work-in-process based on his journals. Used with permission.

avoiding our dreams, we turn away form feeling. We are a nation, and perhaps a world that is turning away from feeling. Our soul calls us to be a poet or a woodcarver. That's all we want, but the culture and our parents ask us to be an accountant because it pays well and is therefore safe. The safe path rather than the path of heart. What are the consequences? I only know them intuitively for myself. When I choose what is safe, I begin to act out of will because feeling is lost as a guide to my behavior. That is what my job involves. It is the safe path. And because so much of my prime time is involved, I get farther and farther from feeling and deeper and deeper into will and routine and doing what I come to think of as my duty, so that when I pass a fifty-year-old juniper that has just been cut to pave the way for some construction I am moved, yes, but way deep inside so that my feelings are an echo, a kind of memory of something that happened long ago.

One of the chain saw workers was artistic and cut off a slice of the trunk about an inch thick and the inside is red like meat, like blood, like heart and this living beauty, this being of storms and winds who has spent his life among us is now gone, and my grief at that passing is only an echo. It was like watching a death on television. No tears because tears and passion are not available on the safe path. They aren't professional.

I carried that slab of tree meat back to my office and then home. What can I do with it? Sand it, oil it, embalm it, give it to a friend? Then I heard D. talk about the cut tree with its stump ground down to the level of the lawn like an amputated limb, and I saw his feeling and it taught me about myself and how buried my own feelings are.

*Chapter Fourteen*

# DREAMS

"Who's got a dream?" I asked.

The dozen dreamers on weekend retreat looked slowly around the circle. For a full minute the only sound was the cheerful popping and crackling of the fire. Thin February sunlight danced through the blinds and shimmered in abstract stripes across Steve's chest. Gradually a dozen gazes rested on him.

Steve cleared his throat. "I had a dream about bricks."

"Will you tell us the dream?" I asked. "Tell it in the present tense, as if it is happening to you right now."

"I dreamed I was standing in front of—"

"I *am* standing in front of—" I coached.

"—I *am* standing in front of some bricks. There are lots of them. Two men tell me to buy the bricks. I buy

them, but I don't know what I'll build. Either a house or
a wall. Then I see some cleared ground and I know that's
where I'll build. There were some other details, but they
don't seem as important."

"What's your best guess about how this dream
relates to your life today?" I asked.

Steve frowned in concentration. "I don't know if this
is right, but . . . my wife died almost four years ago. I'm
ready to start building a new life for myself."

## Why Dreamwork?

Every night when you go to sleep, you script and direct a
movie starring yourself. You create the sets, design the
costumes, order in the props. You play every character.
Your own life dramas are acted out on the stage of your
psyche. You are the only audience. Each performance is
startling in its freshness and creativity.

"Dreams are like letters baked into pies," says
Jungian analyst Clarissa Pinkola Estes. They are answers
to questions we haven't yet thought to ask. Dreams are
like carved ivory Chinese balls that contain increasingly
tinier and more intricately carved balls within them.

They offer us glimpses into the inner workings of
our own minds and hearts. Dreams lift the veil between
the worlds and drop a drawbridge. When you approach
them with reverence and curiosity, they'll help you
understand your life.

Journal work and dreamwork are natural allies. Just
about every program of dream study recommends capturing your dreams in writing. From there you can process
your dream through active imagination and imagery, or

with a therapist or dream group. Or you can use a wide variety of journal techniques and devices.

Dreamwork lets you practice your intuition. When you encounter a truth, there is an unmistakable sensation of knowing. Your skin may tingle, you may gasp sharply, a cartoon lightbulb might explode above you, you may feel "zapped" with a rush of energy. Dreamwork expert Jeremy Taylor calls this sensation the "aha" of recognition and attributes it to memory. In *Where People Fly and Water Runs Uphill* he writes:

> When you discover some true thing about a dream, you are likely to experience the aha of recognition because, in that moment, you *remember*, consciously for the first time, what you *already knew unconsciously* the dream meant at the time it occurred. . . . The aha of recognition . . . is the only reliable touchstone of dream work.

## Paying Attention to the Dream

Dreams feed greedily on attention. The good news about this is that even if you don't remember your dreams now, you'll probably start remembering them once you pledge your attention.

Pay attention to dreams the same way you pay attention to friends: Invite them over. Listen with interest when they talk. Offer your own ideas and opinions. Express appreciation for little gifts.

Invite your dreams in by writing a note in your journal to the Dreamkeeper just before retiring. "Dear Dreamkeeper," you might say. "Tonight I'd like a dream that I can remember and write down. I promise that I'll pay attention to it. Thanks!"

You can get as specific as you want in your request, asking for guidance and clarity about any number of life issues. Dreamkeepers are mighty obliging.

A week or so before I taught the dream journal workshop where Steve told his brick dream, I asked my Dreamkeeper for a dream that I could use as an opening story. That night I received a dream in which an old friend was pregnant. With her was her son, who in the dream was about seven years younger than he was in real life.

I awoke from this dream with a question: *What idea was I gestating about seven years ago that is now ready to be born?*

How was I going to make a story out of this dream? I didn't know.

Two nights before the workshop, I again asked my Dreamkeeper: "Tonight I request a dream that will help me turn the first dream into an opening story. Thanks. Over and out!" The next morning I awoke from a dream in which my father had a heart attack.

There's a tendency to become alarmed when illness or death comes in a dream. But dreams containing scenes of accidents, heart attacks, sudden illnesses or even death aren't usually literal warnings. So I gratefully accepted the *symbol* of my father's heart attack as an answer to my request. Now I had an exact date to work with—the date of my father's mild heart attack seven years earlier!

Within minutes I had uncovered the associations. When my father had his heart attack, I had just begun my own formal study of dreams. I had also just returned from teaching workshops in Tucson and Phoenix. In attendance at the Tucson workshop was a man who had recorded more than five thousand dreams. He had three or four dreams a night and catalogued them all meticulously. Together we brainstormed ways to use the journal process to decipher the messages in dreams.

So the question from my first dream, *What idea was I gestating about seven years ago that is now ready to be born?* was answered: dreams and journals. That became the opening story for my dream journal workshop: how my Dreamkeeper obligingly led me down narrow cobblestone dream-streets to present me with my dream journal origins.

Capture your dream as soon as you awaken. Keep your notebook and pen or a tape recorder right by the bed. Don't move around if you can help it; movement seems to make your dreams leak right out of your brain. If you can't remember every scene or part of the action, just get down what you've got. There seems to be a natural dream-editor in the psyche that deliberately leaves some scenes on the cutting room floor. Don't worry about them. They'll be back if they carry messages you need to receive.

Write your dream in the present tense. This adds immediacy and puts you back in the action. Start by describing the opening scene. How does the dream open? Who's in the scene? What's going on? Replay the dream like a video. Follow the action. What is the mood of the dream? Are there any odd or interesting symbols that don't seem to relate to anything? Follow the dream until it shifts or ends. When you're finished, give your dream a name. Here is the dream Steve told, as he wrote it down.

## THE BUILDING GROUND

In my dream, I am focused narrowly on a pile of bricks before me. I am looking down at them. It is a substantial pile, several hundred, stacked on top of each other to just below my waist. They are a pale brick red, solid and heavy looking. I hear the voices of two men behind me, saying that I should buy the bricks, they are very reasonable now, as it is the end of the building season. I decide I will buy them, but wonder to myself what I will build—a house, or a wall? I never look at, or see, the two men. Instead my gaze now widens to the ground behind the brick pile. I recognize it as the ground I will build on.

### Cracking the Code

Journal dreamwork requires time, commitment, effort and energy. The payoffs are great, but it's an investment. Cracking the Code is a shortcut that efficiently deciphers the basic meaning of a dream and translates it into your own words. It works especially well on short dreams or dream scenes. If your dream is lengthy, like Steve's, play Western Union—collapse it into a telegram of twenty-five words or less. Boil the essence of the dream into the key characters, symbols and actions. Now go back and underline the key nouns and adjectives. These are your code words. Here's how Steve's dream would look:

### THE BUILDING GROUND

I'm standing before a <u>large pile of bricks</u>. <u>Two men</u> tell me to buy them. I don't know what I'll build—a <u>house</u> or a <u>wall</u>. In front of me is <u>cleared ground</u> for building.

Next, assume that every underlined word or phrase has something to do with you or your life. Make a code sheet by writing your code words as a list. Leave yourself some room.

Then take your best guess as to what each code word represents. A best guess is just what it sounds like: a working hypothesis. If you don't have a best guess, try Clustering the code word until you come to an "aha" of recognition. As you arrive at your best guesses, write them on your code sheet.

The *brick pile* is my resources, assets, etc. for living a good life alone or with another.

The *voices* are my supporters and encouragers, unseen because the decision must be mine.

The *house,* of size and shape unknown, is a life shared with a woman.

The *wall* is a protection for my pleasure at independence, and a protection against more pain such as I felt at my wife's death.

The *ground* is my "vacant lot" of possibilities, near other houses, near trees of life.

Now, to crack the code of the dream, rewrite it, substituting your translated code words. Rearrange syntax as needed.

### POSSIBILITIES

I'm standing before my many resources and assets. My supporters encourage me to invest in and own them. I don't know whether to build a life shared with someone else, or a wall of protection against pain and loss. Either way, I will build on my possibilities.

## Exploring the Dream

Cracking the Code gives you the essential overview of the dream. To take its meaning deeper, you can use any number of journal approaches. When you're finished, take another best guess. Steve explored the symbol of the brick pile in a Dialogue.

ME: Hello, brickpile. Why are you in my dream?

BP: I am offering you a reminder that you can put the parts of your life into many possible patterns and forms, according to your creativity and choices.

ME: You're rather daunting to look at in that solid, heavy stacking. It makes me tired just to think of moving all those bricks to my building.

BP: Maybe so, in one part of you. But another part of you can hardly wait to begin creating something out of my present potential.

ME: Would both my possibilities, the house and the wall, offer me some prospect of satisfaction after the labor? Building a wall seems so grim, like a prison wall.

BP: But it could be a garden wall, too, and you could create in it your own pleasure garden.

And you could always build a gate for friends to come through. You could ask the two men who sold you the bricks. They are your friends. I'll tell you something. The building season is *not* "nearly over." You can build any time of year. They gave you a bargain on my bricks because they want to help you. Grow your place as the grass grows.

ME: What if I decide not to build either a house or a wall? What if I decide to build a patio deck with a fountain in the middle—or a summerhouse—or a temple to the trees—or—or—

BP: We're here for you, the ground and the bricks, to do with as you please. It's your life to create as you wish. Just don't build yourself a windowless tomb, please! All of us in your dream wish you well and want you to use us and be with us, so we can be with you in your grassy field where the sun shines.

**Best guess:** I think this dream is about facing the fear and excitement of making new choices about my life, and recognizing the freedom and the power I have to create whatever life I want for myself.

## Acknowledge Yourself

When you've finished your journal work, acknowledge yourself for taking the time to explore your dream. Steve continued his dialogue, but shifted partners to the Dreamkeeper.

ME: Am I right in my interpretation, Dreamkeeper?

DK: You've answered yourself. Didn't you hear
yourself say "Aha"? I heard you.

ME: Thank you, Dreamkeeper, for honoring me
with this dream.

DK: Thank you for honoring me in your dream.
The house door, the garden gate, were both
representations of my openings to the soul.

ME: So I thank myself too.

People who do journal dreamwork report an
interesting phenomenon: Their dreams begin to unfold
like a miniseries over several nights. The next morning
Steve shared another dream.

## BUILD IT AND SHE WILL COME

In a not-quite-awakened state I sce a fine brick house
and a walled garden next to it. The house has
numerous doors and windows, and the garden has a
gate. There is a well-tended lawn all around. As I look,
the face of a woman flickers from window to window,
door to door, and around the garden gate. The face is
glimpsed only for moments, never long enough in one
place for me to see it clearly. I feel uneasy at seeing
such a good house apparently untenanted, with only a
will-of-the-wisp face flickering about. Who will there
be besides me in the house? As I look, I hear a voice
saying: "Build it and she will come." I wake up to the
idea that I must "get my house in order," my life

established as I want it, before I can expect to find the right woman to share it.

Buoyed by the promise of these dreams, Steve commemorated his plan of action in an AlphaPoem based on his angel card of BEAUTY.

### BEAUTY TO BUILD ON

Build it and she will come, whatever and whoever "she" may be.
End the planning and replanning hesitation. Build it
And she will come, the right one for whatever you choose to build.
Unbuilt-on ground yields nothing. Build and your right "she" will come
To
You.

## PICK UP YOUR PEN

- Name your dreams as you would a short story, painting or movie. Keep a separate list of titles; themes may jump out at you.
- Write a Five-Minute Sprint about your first impressions of the dream.
- Cluster the symbols or characters.
- Dialogue with dream symbols or characters.
- Free Write about a particularly elusive symbol or character.
- Write a Captured Moment of a scene from the dream, focusing on the sensory details.

- Use the Identification technique: Go back through your dream and identify the key symbols, characters, etc. Then imagine that you have become the symbol, and so on, and write from the perspective of that symbol. Begin with a simple declarative statement: "I am the yellow baseball cap, and I'm sitting on top of a man's head. I am yellow like lemons and sunshine. I am a baseball cap because I like to be outside in the sun. I am the yellow baseball cap, and I . . ." Stay with this longer than you might think necessary!
- Play Western Union: Rewrite your dream using as few words as possible. Can you get it down to twenty-five words or less? twenty? fifteen?
- Write any kind of a poem about your dream. Focus on the images and the feelings, and let the inner meaning emerge organically. Try an AlphaPoem about a dream symbol.
- Use the Perspectives technique: Write the dream from the perspective of the characters or symbols in the dream—in other words, as if the character/symbol were the "dreamer."
- Paint, draw or sketch your dream or its characters or symbols.
- Write a list of questions raised by the dream. Be as creative and outrageous as you care to be. (Leave yourself a couple of lines between questions.) Then, go back and answer the questions in the space provided. Do this very quickly and without much conscious thought. You'll likely get several "misses" (answers that don't mean anything), but you're also likely to get a few good "hits." Be alert for the "aha"!

*Chapter Fifteen*

# SPIRITUALITY

T here is a story from Jewish mysticism about a
man who received a message in a dream that a
great treasure awaited him. He was to journey at
once to a village many days' travel away, where a sentry
would tell him where to find his treasure.

The man set out immediately, and after long days
and nights of perilous travel he indeed reached the village. Just as the dream foretold, the sentry greeted him
with instructions. "Return to your own village at once,"
the sentry said, "and when you get there, dig under your
hearth."

This was the treasure he had traveled so far to claim?
Disillusioned and embittered, and without resources for
even one night's lodging, the man began the treacherous
journey home. He finally reached his village, bone tired
and despairing. He entered his stone-cold hut. Left only

with the shards of his broken dreams, the man wanted nothing more than to build a fire and warm himself. Yet against all hope he used his last strength to brush the ashes from the hearth and dig beneath it. And there he found his treasure.

I first heard this story years ago, and have since run across it many times in slightly varying forms. It is timeless and universal. Throughout the aeons man sets off on quests to find the elusive treasure that will make him whole and complete. Along the way there are dragons to slay, battles to fight, perils to survive, noble deeds to do. The quest always ends the same way: The answer, the treasure, has been his all along.

For many, the most transformative moment in personal journalkeeping is the awareness that spirituality is available right now, and it can be acknowledged, recognized, created, explored and experienced in the pages of a notebook.

Spirituality and religion are quite different, which is not to say that they are mutually exclusive. In most parts of the world, religion is a cultural heritage as well as a spiritual pursuit. Populations of certain regions, countries or continents are born into prevailing religious orientations. Inherent in any religious orientation is a whole set of values, traditions, directives, philosophies, credos and beliefs.

Spirituality is an internal, personal, individualized relationship with the Source, by whatever name you know it—God, Allah, Christ, Buddha, the Tao, God/dess, Creative Intelligence, Spirit, Higher Power, Infinite Mind. I once knew a man who referred to God as "Howard," which I thought mildly irreverent until he told me that when he learned the Lord's Prayer as a child he thought it said, "Our Father which art in heaven, Howard be thy name."

You can be spiritual without being religious, just as you can be religious without being spiritual. Or you can be both or neither. If you have yearned for deeper meaning and purpose to your life, consider the possibility that a private relationship with your own spirituality could be the treasure buried under your own hearth. Your journal is an excellent place to dig.

## Entering the Silence

Spiritual connection begins with silence. Find a place where you can filter out distractions. When I was small, I took literally the directive from Jesus to "go into the closet and pray." Now I just unplug the phone.

It's nice to clear your space of clutter, but don't wait to try these ideas until you've cleaned your desk. "Power objects" such as stones, shells, crystals, feathers, drums or rattles can help you attain a meditative state, especially if there's a story behind how you found or received them.

If you practice yoga, tai chi, aikido or another movement meditation, you'll find it an excellent place to begin. If not, start out with slow and gentle stretching. This releases tension and grounds you in your body.

Breathe deeply into your abdomen—your center—in full, rhythmic cycles. Not only does this oxygenate your cells, but it is seemingly a necessity for spiritual awareness. As Ira Progoff notes in *The Practice of Process Meditation*:

> The connection between breath and spirit is a fact that has been widely recognized in religious history.

Wherever people have worked seriously with spiritual disciplines, they have noted the close relationship between the movement of the breath and the quality of inner experience. . . . The regulation of the breath plays an important role in balancing the inner and outer aspects of a person's life. In particular, the quieting of the self is related to the stabilizing of the breathing, especially in the way that it helps neutralize the hold that habits have on us. It helps us establish at least a degree of freedom from being controlled by our conscious ego.

## Affirmations and Mantras

Affirmations are powerful, positive messages stated or written in the present tense, as if they were already true. Repetition of affirmations many, many times helps create new pathways in the belief system. It isn't necessary for you to believe the statement in the affirmation. It is, however, important that you have a desire that the statement in the affirmation be true for you, now or in the future.

Writing affirmations has an even more powerful effect than speaking them, because it involves concrete cognitive activity. Writing grounds affirmations into present-moment reality.

Most powerful of all is to speak the affirmation aloud as you write it. This gives you a triple experience: visual, kinesthetic (motor/feeling) and auditory.

Keep affirmations brief, simple and powerful. You can discern the best affirmations for yourself by completing in several ways the Sentence Stem, "I wish I were . . ."

or "I wish I could . . ." Go through your lists and select the two or three responses that evoke an emotional response. Then reconstruct the desire as an affirmation, substituting "I am . . ." for ". . . I were" or ". . . I could."

Divide your page vertically. On the left side, write your affirmation: *I am creative and productive.* Across from it on the right side, write whatever your internal voices say in response: *No, you're not.* Keep going on the left: *I am creative and productive.* And on the right: *What a joke!* Keep going until you harmonize the affirmation with your inner voice. Lasting change happens over many sessions; short-term impact can be derived within a page or two.

Repeatedly writing an affirmation such as "The guiding voice of wisdom speaks within my heart" or "I am quiet and serene" is an excellent warm-up for a "soul write" session.

Progoff's work with written process meditation suggests seven-syllable "mantra/crystals" drawn from the context of the individual's life history. "In making the mantra/crystal, we are seeking merely to put a small, representative piece [of the experience] into words in a way that will recall us to the atmosphere of the original experience," he writes.

There is apparently a factor of inner wisdom that expresses itself at the depth of human beings whenever the circumstances are right for it, and this factor seems to have a direct affinity for the seven-syllable mantra/crystals. I infer that the seven-syllable form and rhythm reflects an inherent cycle in the natural world, and therefore it easily comes into harmony with the principle of inner wisdom that is present at the depth levels of the human psyche.

In addition to the prescribed length, Progoff suggests that the chosen phrase be smooth and rhythmic "so that we can easily speak and repeat them under our breath . . . without conscious effort or thought." The mantra/crystal should correspond to your individual breath pattern so that you can fit the entire phrase into one cycle of breathing in and breathing out. Progoff emphasizes the benefit of gerunds (verbs ending in -*ing*) because of their inherent movement and flow.

The construction of mantra/crystals from your own life experience is both complex and subtle, and I refer you to *The Practice of Process Meditation* for the full treatment. The essential question to ask is, Where does it place me in my inner space? If your mantra/crystal reflects a statement, idea, conscious belief or doctrine, it will draw you into the mental realm. "Choose an image, therefore, a symbol, a metaphor, since these can move about naturally in the twilight range like fish in the oceanic waters." Some examples from Progoff's work follow.

- Letting the Self become still
- Holding the stillness within
- Feeling the movement of life
- The river flows to the sea
- Knowing the goodness of God
- Feeling the love of the Lord
- Feeling the pain of my life
- The morning song of the birds
- I and my Father are One

Keep your journal open before you as you silently speak your mantra/crystal to the rhythm of your breath. Notice any images, symbols, feelings, colors or awarenesses. Write them down in simple words or phrases: "Flash of orange/gold in dark tunnel." "Peace, calm, tears." "Ocean wave." You can open your eyes just slightly enough to see, or you can try holding your left index finger (if you're right-handed) lightly above the tip of your pen and writing with your eyes closed.

## The Journal as Meditative Act

Writing becomes a meditation when you bring your total awareness and gratitude to the act. Practice this by first placing your entire awareness and mindfulness on entering the writing session through the tools we have already discussed. When you have created a receptive space in your environment, bring your attention to your journal. Become aware that Spirit moving through you is actively creating something that is unique in all the world and that did not exist even a moment ago. Michael speaks to this phenomenon.

When I write in my journal, I affix ink onto paper, resulting in a visual display which can be returned to over and over again. I have begun to ask myself the questions: What do I want to make now? What might I want to see/read in the future? Is what I am creating now in the service of my wants? And so I have been attending to not only content, but also form, and sprinkling my pages with symbols which remind me of the sacredness of my practice: hearts, simple mandalas, the star of David, exclamation points, question marks and spirals. I've become freer with paper, too, double-spacing for visual effect and occasionally just leaving a page with a word or two on it—a statement of simplicity and significance.

When you feel ready, take a deep breath and begin a written meditation. It doesn't matter where you start, but if you need a jumping-off place, imagine yourself in a beautiful, secluded, serene place in nature. Or remember a time when you experienced a moment of grace or bliss, as Bob did.

> I'm watching Tessa walk down the trail. I sense there is something different going on in her, as she is walking with hands held open to the world. In a few minutes she stops, looking imperceptibly moist-eyed. She speaks a few words, then begins crying. She describes feeling open to the universe, and just *being*. We hug, and I ask if it means, in part, not thinking or doing. She agrees. As I write this now, I'm getting teary myself. How numinous it is to be in the Tao, how moving to see another person experience it. To be able to suspend judgment, to just *be*, how extraordinary! (Bob)

Allow yourself to simply write. Suspend judgment about whether you're doing it right. If you come to a natural pause in your writing, go back and reread what you've already written. Your writing will often spontaneously continue.

## Unseen Companions

Last winter, in the midst of the darkest nights of the year, I experienced a dark night of the soul. My faith was seriously tested; I struggled with a profound sense of alienation from God. Like the psalmist David, "I cry by day, but thou dost not answer; and by night, but find no rest." (Psalms 22:2)

Dark night or no, life goes on. One day I stopped by the neighborhood bookstore to pick up a few Christmas gifts. Twenty minutes later, loaded chest-high with books, I headed to the sales counter. The aisles were narrow, the crowds were jostling, and suddenly a book came sailing through the air and landed face-up in my arms.

"I'm terribly sorry!" cried the woman with whom I'd collided. "Let me put that away!" As she reached for the book, I glanced down. On the cover was Abbott Handerson Thayer's painting *Angel*, which I remembered from my college humanities class. The book was called *Ask Your Angels*. I laughed out loud. "That's okay," I told the apologetic "angel" who caused the book to fly into my waiting heart. "I'll just buy it."

Angels, guides, muses, the spirits of beloved ones who have passed on, the Holy Ghost, patron saints, Christ Consciousness, nature, devas, the Soul, the Wise Ones, intuition, Higher Self . . . all of these are unseen companions whose support and guidance are available for the asking. The journal is a wonderfully eclectic melting pot for unseen companions. It doesn't matter what you call them, or if you call them anything at all. Just ask for their guidance. Then wait for the answer. Write whatever comes.

It may seem foreign, odd or unsettling to communicate with unseen companions, but Alma Daniel and her coauthors of *Ask Your Angels* assure us it's perfectly natural:

Contact and conversation with your angel is filled with all the tenderness, love and wonderment of discovering a best friend. Talking with angels is an entirely natural relationship, although over the centuries it's become obscured by the belief that if you can't see something or touch it—it isn't real.

The Inner Wisdom dialogue is the communication technique of choice for most experienced spiritual journalkeepers. Allow plenty of time; the dialogue often unfolds in waves or layers interspersed with periods of silence. Preparing a list of questions may make entry more smooth. Usually after a few exchanges, the dialogue will find its own direction.

## Written Prayer and Meditation

A written prayer or devotional journal not only strengthens faith but also serves as a permanent testament to your spiritual evolution. You may wish to prepare by reading a sacred text such as the Bible, the Koran, the Book of Changes, the Course in Miracles textbook, or another guide. Write or summarize the passage in your journal. Be sure to date your entry.

As you meditate on the passage, allow questions or prayers to come to you. When you feel moved to write, do so. Speak your word to God. Listen for guidance. Note the messages you receive.

## Soul Write

When you are writing from your spiritual center, it feels effortless. Words flow freely. Storytelling becomes natural and fluid. You may feel as if you are in an altered state of consciousness, where time is elastic and acuity is sharpened. You may feel expansive and connected to the unity of all things. There is often a sense of gratitude, peace of mind and clarity. It is as if you are writing from your soul.

Often this state of "soul write" comes after an experience of transformation or spiritual awakening, as it did for Steve. Rest assured that you will know it when you experience it; and rest assured you can experience it. As the philosopher Paul Williams said, "Be honest. Be present. Be modest and courageous. Spirit will take care of the rest."

On March 17, 1990, I found myself wrapped in the peace and love of the Highest Spirit for the first time in my life. It was a little more than a year after my wife's suicide. In constant pain from an illness doctors could not diagnose, she ended her life as she had lived it: quietly, neatly, efficiently, decisively. I could not recover from her death in the same way. Only a year later was I beginning to sift its meaning.

A first step was a weekend retreat with my local men's center. The leader, Tom, took us through the ritual of the sweat lodge. I was fearful of it physically, as my medication made me especially liable to be overcome by heat. The act of stripping myself naked in the open air of day, in front of a group of men I was only starting to know, made me feel vulnerable emotionally as well.

The heat, the darkness, the steam of water on rocks, the chatter of Tom's rattles and the screaming of the men had a powerful impact on me. I thought I was all right when I left the sweat lodge for the last time. But when I stepped out into the cool air, I staggered. I suddenly found myself stretched out on the ground, dazed and weak. I had fainted.

The first thing my mind's voice said to me was, "Well, Steve, this is as low as you can go." I was flat on my back in the dirt, totally naked, smeared with sweat and mud from the lodge, and too feeble even to sit up.

From earlier experiences, especially of my father, I expected to be derided for weakness. But it didn't happen that way. Instead, all I felt was the compassion and concern of those men around me. I could suddenly realize that not all men were like my father. I remember in particular how Tom lay beside me, talking quietly until I was able to sit up and make my slow way to the lake.

There I did not so much feel the water as regain a sense of vision I had as I lay on the ground in the moment before my eyes opened. I remembered feeling I was, in some way beyond anything I could sense, in the presence of something tremendously powerful and tremendously loving, who would never let me be lost. I remembered receiving, not through the senses, the message of a single repeated word: "Forgiveness, forgiveness."

Until that day, I had never considered myself capable of spirituality, of receiving a divine love. After all, I had known nothing of a father's love in my childhood. But since March 17, 1990 I have known it is there for me forever, in the human realm and beyond.

What did the repeated word mean? Someone or something's forgiveness of me? My forgiveness of one or more figures in my life? I'm still working on that. I know I have reached a sad forgiveness of my father and mother. I am working on forgiveness of other wounding people in my life. I have forgiven—or given over—the hurt my wife caused by withdrawing from life without even a goodbye to me.

I have proceeded in many new directions in the past few years. In all of them I have been aware of the guidance of my Highest Spirit, and the love sent to me through human friends.

I continue my new life, blessed with the sustaining spirituality that began in one moment, in the mud by the lake, that day in 1990. I continually wonder how the change came about, and why it came when it did. But I don't demand an answer. Tom said to me, "It came because you were ready for it." Another friend called it the mystery of grace. I have only to accept it. I am blessed. I am blessed.

## PICK UP YOUR PEN

- Sentence Stems:
  - Religion is . . .
  - Spirituality is . . .
  - Faith is . . .
  - My unseen companions . . .
- Reflect on an object that carries spiritual significance

for you. If possible, touch or look at it. Write about
what it means to you and how you received it.

- Write powerful, present-tense affirmations. Divide your
  page vertically. Write your affirmation on the left and
  your internal response on the right. Continue until you
  notice a shift in your self-talk.
- From a particularly meaningful experience or writing,
  select a phrase that can be converted into a seven-syllable, rhythmic mantra/crystal. Use your mantra/crystal
  as an entry point to meditation or soul write.
- Meditate on a passage from a holy book. Write your
  impressions as they come to you.
- Write about an experience with an unseen companion.
- Write a Dialogue with your Inner Wisdom.
- Have you had a moment of spiritual transformation?
  How did it come about? How has your life been different since?
- A peaceful heart is a good place to start. Each time you
  sit down for a session of "soul write," first count your
  blessings. Whom and what do you love? For what do
  you forgive others? For what do you forgive yourself?
  For what are you grateful?

*Part Three*

# RESOURCES

# GUIDELINES FOR JOURNAL GROUPS

*B*y its very nature, journal writing is a solitary activity. No matter how enjoyable or beneficial, reflective writing can be a lonely journey. Connecting with others through a journal group has many benefits. You get all the advantages of your own reflective process. You have company and support while you explore your life issues. You can share your writing and receive feedback and comments. And you learn from hearing the writings of others in the group. The group format also offers useful structure and incentive if your writing slacks off during busy times, as it does for almost all of us.

## Finding Members

Many journal groups start spontaneously when a few friends decide to get together and write. If you belong to a weekly men's group, you might suggest that one meeting a month be dedicated to process writing. Or perhaps your family could set aside an evening a month for community writing and sharing.

Other ways to find members: Ask your friends. Ask bookstores if they'd help sponsor a writing group and donate meeting space. Put a notice up on the bulletin board of your church, athletic club, apartment complex, laundromat. Think carefully before you put out the word to your office or work crowd. Will you (or others) feel hesitant or awkward disclosing personal thoughts and feelings to colleagues you work with?

Do you want just men in your group, or men and women together? If you want a mixed group, ask your women friends, wife, girlfriend, sister to attend and bring their boyfriends, husbands, brothers, friends.

The ideal group size is five to eight. However, not everyone will come every time, so shoot for eight to twelve members.

## Ground Rules

Ground rules are the basic agreements all the members make about how the group will operate. Although many ground rules can be established by consensus, rules concerning confidentiality, sharing and feedback are non-negotiable.

*Confidentiality.* It is imperative that everyone in the group agree to respect privacy and confidentiality of all members. In its strictest sense, this calls for an agreement that nothing that takes place within the group will be shared outside the group. This helps individual members develop trust that the group is a safe place to reveal and explore sensitive issues and feelings. Some groups relax the concept of strict confidentiality into one in which group members agree that the group process can be shared with others as long as individual anonymity is protected. This is more realistic than strict confidentiality, because people tend to share about their own experience or writing with partners or friends. However, anyone else's experience or writing should be off limits outside the group unless you have his/her express permission.

*Sharing.* There is something very powerful about hearing your own words in your own voice in the company of others who carefully listen. Reading your own writing out loud, and hearing the writings of others, are two dynamics that make journal groups so effective. Therefore, sharing should be encouraged. But sharing is always optional. The right to privacy in the journal always takes precedence, and no one should ever be made to feel pressured or challenged to share.

This can get tricky in the beginning, because almost everybody experiences an initial shyness in reading their journals aloud. Once the ice is broken, this shyness usually melts away. As the organizer of the group, be a role model by volunteering to read your own writing. The space between the "comfort zone" and the "chaos zone" is the "stretch zone." Without pushing, encourage group members to stretch into the risk of sharing their writing.

*Feedback.* It is absolutely imperative that group members agree to accept what's offered without criticism (literary or otherwise), advice, or problem-solving. There is much to be said for silent reception, or an agreement to receive sharings with a nod, a "ho" or a "thank you." Such silent reception takes the pressure off the group to come up with comments. It also leaves the privilege of interpreting the writing's meaning with the writer, where it rightfully belongs. Additionally, it avoids blurring the boundaries between what got said (expression of experience) and how it got said (technical skill). So agree to silent reception as a ground rule for at least the beginning stages of the group.

Later, when members are comfortable with each other and with silent reception you can add experience-centered feedback to this ground rule. Experience-centered feedback shares what was evoked in the listener as the writing was offered. Remember, no criticism (literary or otherwise), no advice, no problem-solving. Phrases like "As I listen, I feel . . ." or "Right now I'm aware of . . ." or "Your writing evokes in me . . ." are good openers.

*Other ground rules.* Other agreements include negotiating how often and where and for how long the group will meet (biweekly or monthly meetings are easier to schedule than weekly; two to three hours is a good length), the level of commitment of group members, how leadership will be handled, what the basic format will be, how group time will be spent, and whether new people can join the group once it gets going. Ground rules like these are discussed thoroughly in Bill Kauth's book *A Circle of Men: The Original Manual for Men's Support Groups.*

## Leadership

Most journal groups work best with shared leadership, where group members take turns moderating and/or hosting the group. If you meet in each other's homes, the moderator and host can be the same person. The moderator's job is to choose the writing topics and introduce them, be the timekeeper, invite sharings, and keep the group moving. In addition to providing a reasonably comfortable and private meeting place, the host may also provide refreshments.

A journal group isn't supposed to be a group therapy session. Although members often attain insight into and clarity about life issues, the purpose of the group isn't problem-solving, fixing people, or giving advice. Each member has his/her own answers waiting to be revealed. Let the journal do its work.

## Format

A suggested journal group format includes three phases: warm-up, process writing, and closing reflection.

*Warm-Up.* Use quick, casual Sentence Stems or Five-Minute Sprints to stretch the journal muscles. Some suggestions:

- Best thing/worst thing about the day
- Funniest thing that's happened to you lately
- World event you're most interested in today
- Most exciting event of your week or day
- Five ideas for future warm-up topics

Go around the circle and share the warm-up writing as a group check-in. This is a very good time to use silent reception so that you avoid getting sidetracked.

*Process Writing.* This book is loaded with ideas for process writing. Any of the Pick Up Your Pen suggestions will do fine. Select writing topics that are relevant to most, if not all, of the group members. Take examples, explanations and directions directly from this book. Set a timer or stopwatch for ten to twenty minutes. Allow more time as you advance up the journal ladder. At the end of the writing period, ask for sharings. Remind the group about silent reception and experience-centered feedback.

*Closing reflection.* About fifteen or twenty minutes before the group time is up, shift into closing reflection. This is a Five-Minute Sprint that addresses any or all of the following Springboards:

- What have I learned about myself tonight?
- What has affected me the most tonight?
- Is there action to take? If so, what is it?
- What is my next step?

Go around the circle and share closing reflections to adjourn the group. Your group may also want to have a closing ritual such as a group hug or yell.

## Handling Feelings

It's normal, natural and common for deep and unexpected

feelings to surface during process writing and sharing. It's sometimes also uncomfortable and embarrassing to begin to cry as you write or read or listen. Everyone will handle this in his/her own way, but here are some suggestions.

Writing deeply and reading your own words aloud will often connect you to grief, love, sentimentality or joy. Your eyes may fill with tears and your voice may crack or break. Keep breathing! If you need to pause while reading, just do so. The group will wait. Continue reading when you're ready. If you can't continue, ask someone to finish reading for you.

It's a good idea to have a box or two of tissues in the room. Don't make a big deal out of passing them at the first sign of a sniffle or a choke; set as a ground rule that anyone who needs a tissue can get up and get one or ask that the box be passed. Placing the box in the middle of the circle at the beginning of group helps establish a matter-of-fact attitude toward the normalcy of tears when doing emotional work. People have different reactions to being patted or touched while they're crying; sometimes it's a distraction that takes the individual out of the immediacy of the moment, and at other times it's a welcome connection to compassion. When in doubt, ask.

If anger surfaces while you write, let the group know how you're feeling. Excuse yourself for a brisk walk around the block, a few minutes of quiet time, or another type of time out if you need to. Reflect on what triggered the anger.

If you're very uncomfortable with your own emotions or those of others, observe your own thoughts and feelings. Jot down notes about your thoughts, judgments, feelings and internal messages. One at a time, track them back to their roots. Chances are you'll find that you're responding to something you learned or assimilated in childhood, like "Big boys don't cry." Take advantage of the opportunity to reflect on your internalized beliefs about emotions and their expressions. Challenge the belief or message. Replace it with a more updated one, like "Tears are natural and healthy."

## A Circle of Men

Bill Kauth's *A Circle of Men* is a practical, hands-on, user-friendly manual for organizing and leading men's support groups. It's loaded with suggestions for finding members, establishing consistency, creating a safe space, listening and talking, creating ritual and much more.

## MIGHTIER THAN THE SWORD Workshops

I have trained selected individuals to offer *Mightier Than the Sword* men's journal workshops in their own communities. For a list of instructors in your area or to request information on the instructor training program, write or fax.

Through the writings of the men in this book, you've tasted what it's like to gather in community and share the journal experience. It's powerful. I recommend it.

# SOME GOOD BOOKS

JOURNALS AND WRITING

- Adams, Kathleen. *Journal to the Self: 22 Paths to Personal Growth*. New York: Warner Books, 1990. A comprehensive basic book featuring a technique approach to journal writing and a focus on the therapeutic benefits of reflective writing.
- Adams, Kathleen. *The Way of the Journal: A Journal Therapy Workbook for Healing*. Lutherville, MD: Sidran Press, 1993. A ten-step "quick and easy" method featuring the journal ladder, in a well-designed workbook format.
- Hageseth, Christian. *Thirteen Moon Journal: A Psychiatrist's Journey Toward Inner Peace*. Fort Collins, CO: Berwick Publishing, 1991. The author, a self-described "analog man in a digital world," guides the

reader through a year-long cycle (thirteen moons) of his
life.

- Mack, Karen, and Eric Skjei. *Overcoming Writing Blocks.*
  Los Angeles: J. P. Tarcher, 1979. For fifteen years this has
  been my favorite book on writing for an audience. More
  than fifty seasoned, reliable, effective unblocking techniques.
- Mallon, Thomas. *A Book of One's Own: People and Their
  Diaries.* London: Penguin Books, 1986. A witty and
  wide-ranging exploration of the art and history of diary
  writing.
- Palmer, Laura. *Shrapnel in the Heart: Letters and
  Remembrances From the Vietnam Veterans Memorial.*
  New York: Random House, 1987. A collection of letters
  and poems left at "the wall" in Washington, D.C., and an
  exploration of the cultural phenomenon of active
  remembrance of those lost in the Vietnam War.
- Pennebaker, James. *Opening Up: The Healing Power of
  Confiding in Others.* New York: Avon Books, 1990.
  Research from a leading psychologist suggests that writ-
  ing really is good for you: Writing about emotionally dif-
  ficult subjects causes immune system functioning and
  overall capacity to withstand stress to be elevated.
- Progoff, Ira. *The Practice of Process Meditation: The
  Intensive Journal Way to Spiritual Experience.* New York:
  Dialogue House, 1980. This companion volume to *At a
  Journal Workshop* (recently rereleased by J. P. Tarcher)
  opens a path to "depth beyond doctrines" by using writing meditation as spiritual practice.
- Rico, Gabriele. *Pain and Possibility: Writing Your Way
  Through Personal Crisis.* Los Angeles: J. P. Tarcher, 1991.
  A warmly personal guide to using natural writing tech-
  niques to heal emotional pain, from a leader in whole-
  brained creative process.
- Solly, Richard, and Roseann Lloyd. *JourneyNotes: Writing
  for Recovery and Spiritual Growth.* New York:

Harper/Hazelden, 1989. Creative writing and journal ideas for people in twelve-step recovery programs.
* Wakefield, Dan. *The Story of Your Life: Writing a Spiritual Autobiography.* A step-by-step approach to exploring your past and understanding your present.

## Men's Psychology and the Men's Movement

* Allen, Marvin. *Angry Men, Passive Men: Understanding the Roots of Men's Anger and Moving Beyond It* (published in hardcover as *In the Company of Men*). New York: Random House, 1993. A down-to-earth guide to healing the emotional problems common to all men.
* Friel, John. *The Grown-Up Man.* Deerfield Beach, FL: Health Communications, 1991. The author leads a journey into a world where men and women respect themselves and each other and where qualities of integrity and honor reign.
* Harding, Christopher, ed. *Wingspan: Inside the Men's Movement.* New York: St. Martin's Press, 1992. A collection of essays and photographs from fifteen years of the men's press.
* Hicks, Robert. *The Masculine Journey: Understanding the Six Stages of Manhood.* Colorado Springs: Navpress Publishing, 1993. A biblical scholar and counselor explores the roots of masculinity.
* Kauth, Bill. *A Circle of Men: The Original Manual for Men's Support Groups.* New York: St. Martin's Press, 1992. A step-by-step manual on how to start a men's group, find new members, solve group problems, and create rituals and activities that promote honesty, self-disclosure and fun.
* Keen, Sam. *Fire in the Belly: On Being a Man.* New York: Bantam Books, 1991. The groundbreaking men's book that confronts outdated rites of passage and suggests

new routes to a self-actualized, spiritually grounded masculinity.

- Kivel, Paul. *Men's Work: How to Stop the Violence That Tears Our Lives Apart.* New York: Ballantine Books, 1992. A revolutionary and vitally important work that gives men back the power and responsibility they need to unlearn the lessons of control and aggression.
- Lee, John. *At My Father's Wedding: Reclaiming Our True Masculinity.* New York: Bantam Books, 1991. A groundbreaking book about the "father wound" and the pain men bear because of it.
- Lee, John, and Bill Stott. *Facing the Fire: Experiencing and Expressing Anger Appropriately.* New York: Bantam Books, 1993. A practical, straightforward and much-needed book on how to confront and express anger in constructive, creative and nonviolent ways.
- Morley, Patrick. *The Man in the Mirror: Solving the 24 Problems Men Face.* Brentwood, TN: Wolgemuth & Hyatt, 1989. A Christian perspective for men grappling with the pressure and stress of everyday life. Each chapter concludes with focus questions that can be explored in the journal.

PERSONAL MYTHOLOGY AND ARCHETYPES

- Bolen, Jean Shinoda. *Gods in Everyman: A New Psychology of Men's Lives and Loves.* New York: Harper & Row, 1989. The powerful inner and personal patterns, or archetypes, that shape men's personalities, careers and relationships, told from a Jungian perspective through the stories of mythological gods.
- Keen, Sam, and Anne Valley-Fox. *Your Mythic Journey: Finding Meaning in Your Life Through Writing and Storytelling.* Los Angeles: J. P. Tarcher, 1989 (originally published 1973). An introduction to personal mythology

that explores the story lines of your personal, cultural and sociological history.

- Larsen, Stephen. *The Mythic Imagination: Your Quest for Meaning Through Personal Mythology*. New York: Bantam Books, 1990. Through the use of dreams, stories and creative exercises, the author leads a tour of the "living landscape" of the psyche. The section on Conscious Mythmaking includes ideas for journal exploration as well as good discussions of maskmaking and sandplay.
- Richardson, Donald. *Greek Mythology for Everyone: Legends of the Gods and Heroes*. New York: Avenel Books, 1989. Contemporary and witty retelling of Greek myths and legends, intricately woven into a fierce, sensual and eloquent tapestry of archetypal lore.

## More Good Books

- Cameron, Julia. *The Artist's Way: A Spiritual Path to Higher Creativity*. New York: Tarcher/Perigree Books, 1992. A comprehensive, guided twelve-week program to overcome creative blocks and recover inspiration.
- Davis, Martha; Eshelman, Elizabeth Robbins; and Matthew McKay. *The Relaxation and Stress Reduction Workbook*. Oakland, CA: New Harbinger Publications, 1988. Simple, concise, step-by-step directions for the management of stress, anxiety, fear, unwanted thoughts, burnout, insomnia and irritability.
- Gendler, J. Ruth. *The Book of Qualities*. New York: HarperCollins, 1988. The author personifies seventy-five emotions and qualities by describing them as people with histories, quirks, personalities and habits. A gentle and clever introduction to feelings.
- Taylor, Jeremy. *Where People Fly and Water Runs Uphill*. New York: Warner Books, 1992. How to use dreams to tap the wisdom of the unconscious, from one of the most articulate dreamworkers of our time.

# ABOUT THE AUTHOR

KATHLEEN ADAMS, M.A. L.P.C., is a licensed psychotherapist, author, educator and internationally acclaimed pioneer in journal therapy. In 1985 she founded The Center for Journal Therapy in Denver. Kay is the Co-Director of the Centre for Journal Writing in Toronto and is on the faculties of many institutes, colleges, and conferences. She is the author of *Journal to the Self* and a workbook, *The Way of the Journal*.

# PLEASE WRITE!

Dear Kay:
- ❏ I liked your book! My comments are enclosed.
- ❏ Please add me to your mailing list and send:
    - ❏ A sample issue of your newsletter
    - ❏ Your workshop and teaching schedule
    - ❏ A list of Certified Instructors in my area
    - ❏ Info on journal software
    - ❏ Info about the Instructor Certification Training
    - ❏ Info about the National Association for Poetry Therapy
- ❏ I'm enclosing a journal entry or two.
- ❏ Connect me with other men who journal.
- ❏ RUSH your response.
- ❏ I've included my name, address and fax number.

SEND TO:
The Center for Journal
Therapy
Attn: MTS
P.O. Box 963
Arvada, CO 80001
fax 303-421-1255

IN CANADA:
Centre for Journal Writing
Attn: MTS
12 Grovetree Road
Etobicoke, ONT, CAN M9V
2Y2
fax 416-744-3127